Jung's Word Association Experiment

This manual is the long-awaited definitive and essential guide to training, research and practice of Jung's Word Association Experiment, both in clinical practice and beyond the consulting room.

Carefully redesigned by training analysts, examiners and researchers at the C. G. Jung Institute Zurich in consultation with a multi-disciplinary group of international authorities, this manual will enable multi-disciplinary practice and discourse while supporting a research/practitioner model. WAE grabs the spotlight as a therapeutic instrument remodelled to deliver measurable patient benefit. Bridging the worlds of empirical science and the depths of the human psyche, this book provides a platform for research into psychotherapeutic effectiveness and efficacy. The incorporation of Jung's mature reflections, and of contemporary research, teaching and practice provides solid new insights to support established and innovative practice as well as further scientific research.

This is a valuable new resource written for students and for the continuing professional development of analysts, academics and fellow professionals.

John O'Brien is an accredited training Jungian psychoanalyst engaged in lecturing, research writing and supporting individuals, groups and the wider community through the processes of individuation.

Nada O'Brien is an accredited training Jungian analyst in private practice, working with individuals and groups. She is a lecturer, researcher and published author.

Jung's Word Association Experiment
Manual for Training and Practice

John O'Brien and Nada O'Brien

LONDON AND NEW YORK

Designed cover image: A creation of John O'Brien (2025)

First published 2025
by Routledge
4 Park Square, Milton Park, Abingdon, Oxon OX14 4RN

and by Routledge
605 Third Avenue, New York, NY 10158

Routledge is an imprint of the Taylor & Francis Group, an informa business

© 2025 John O'Brien and Nada O'Brien

The right of John O'Brien and Nada O'Brien to be identified as authors of this work has been asserted in accordance with sections 77 and 78 of the Copyright, Designs and Patents Act 1988.

All rights reserved. No part of this book may be reprinted or reproduced or utilised in any form or by any electronic, mechanical, or other means, now known or hereafter invented, including photocopying and recording, or in any information storage or retrieval system, without permission in writing from the publishers.

Trademark notice: Product or corporate names may be trademarks or registered trademarks, and are used only for identification and explanation without intent to infringe.

British Library Cataloguing-in-Publication Data
A catalogue record for this book is available from the British Library

ISBN: 978-1-032-71656-5 (hbk)
ISBN: 978-1-032-71655-8 (pbk)
ISBN: 978-1-032-71657-2 (ebk)

DOI: 10.4324/9781032716572

Typeset in Times New Roman
by Apex CoVantage, LLC

Contents

About the authors ix

1 Jung's Word Association Experiment 1
JOHN O'BRIEN

Introduction 1
Jung's early experimental research methods 1
The discovery of complexes 2
Working definitions 3
Practical applications in training 3
References 4
Additional Resources 4

2 WAE training for student analysts and practitioners 6
JOHN O'BRIEN

Training rationale and overview 6
Scientific framework 6
Function of the WAE as a 'rite of passage' in training 7
Developing the character of the analyst 7
Learning outcomes 7
Additional Resources 8

3 Preparing for the AE 9
JOHN O'BRIEN

Step-by-step learning guide 9
Uses of the AE 10
Research ethics protocol 11
Letter of introduction example 11
Structure of the AE final exam document 12

4 Taking the anamnesis 14
JOHN O'BRIEN

Introduction 14
Guidance 14
Aims 15
Practical guide 15
Example introduction 15
Example anamnesis 16
Special characteristics of the Jungian anamnesis 19
References 20

5 AE protocol 21
JOHN O'BRIEN

Example of a completed AE template 21
How to administer the AE using the template 23
First 'administration' meeting 23
How to organise the data for analysis 25
Conclusion 32
References 32
Additional Resources 32

6 The context interview 33
JOHN O'BRIEN

Preparing for the context interview 33
Guidance notes on the context interview 33
Using video/audio recordings 34
Interviewing method 34
Example of context interview 35
Relevant research 41
References 42
Additional Resources 42

7 Map of complexes 43
NADA O'BRIEN

Map of complexes 43
Process of articulating the map 43
References 48

8 Building an interpretation hypothesis and therapeutic use of WAE 49
NADA O'BRIEN, JOHN O'BRIEN

Building an interpretation hypothesis 49
Therapeutic use of WAE 51
References 52

9 Behind words: Developmental perspective 53
NADA O'BRIEN

Behind words 53
Development of the senses of self 53
Behind words: Remembering Sophia 56
References 56

10 WAE examination document: Example 57
NADA O'BRIEN

Anamnesis 58
Description of the experimental setting, initial counter-transference 60
Analysis of the feedback after the first part of the experiment and data from the unconscious 62
Analysis of protocol 63
Context interview 74
Interpretation hypothesis 81
Indications for the therapeutic work 83
Reflections on the AE experience for the candidate's individuation process 83
Appendix: borderline personality disorder short description and symptoms 84
References 84

11 The Word Association Experiment and the DSM/ICD categories 85
JOHN O'BRIEN

Overview of ICD and DSM 85
Further background to the DSM 87
Summary of key features 88
WAE and links to DSM and ICD categories 88
Example 89
Association Experiment 90
Use with transdiagnostic classification 91
Summary 92
References 93

12 Research 94
JOHN O'BRIEN

Introduction 94
Humanistic and general psychotherapy 96
Common factor models in psychotherapy research 98
Current WAE/WAT research approaches 99
Artificial intelligence (AI) 99
Clinical implications 100
Reflections 100
References 101

13 Further thoughts 103
JOHN O'BRIEN

Jung's opus as context for the Word Association Experiment 103
The fractal quality of Jung's approach 105
An elaboration of artificial intelligence 106
An elaboration of neuroscience and psychiatry 106
An elaboration of connection and interpretation derived from the Word Association Experiment 109
References 110

Glossary of terms *111*
JOHN O'BRIEN

Introduction 111
Glossary 111
References 132

Appendix 1 Note on further research: Recursive analysis *134*
Appendix 2 100-word list *140*
Appendix 3 Global Assessment of Functioning (GAF) scale *142*

Index *144*

About the authors

John O'Brien, PhD, is an accredited analyst, training analyst and Research Committee member at the C. G. Jung Institute Kusnacht, Switzerland). In parallel with his career as a psychoanalyst, John is dual qualified and experienced in leadership consulting and culture in major corporations and institutions in Europe, UK and the USA. John is a published author and leader of certified advanced programmes of education, training and group analysis (www.cgjungcentre.com), Chair of the International Association for Jungian Coaching and Consulting (www.iajcc.org) and Director of CG Jung Centre (www.cgjungcentre.com).

Nada O'Brien, PhD, is an accredited Jungian analyst (C. G. Jung Institute Kusnacht, Switzerland), supervisor, university professor and a consultant. For more than 20 years, she worked with individuals, groups and organisations. She is a leader of personal and professional development programmes, educational and training courses and dream groups (www.cgjungcentre.com). She is a published author and a researcher in the fields of analytic psychology, leadership, organisational transformation, education, music, sports and human development. Nada is also Co-founder and Director of Training at iajcc.org and Co-director of the CG Jung Centre (www.cgjungcentre.com).

1 Jung's Word Association Experiment

John O'Brien

Introduction

More than a century ago, a great scientific enquiry into the nature of the human psyche was taking place. Today, it could be said that despite the collective educational and psychotherapeutic knowledge gathered over the course of 125 years, we may not have made as much progress as our ancestors would have wished for us. Perhaps as a global psychotherapeutic community we have failed. Perhaps many of us still find ourselves 'in search of' a soul'. But much as we may grieve the ills of our times, we continue our craft or art 'by singing light'.

The Association Experiment is central to the theory and practice of Jungian psychotherapy and psychoanalysis, otherwise known as 'analytical psychology'. In 1957, more than half a century after his first experiments, Jung declared that he had long since stopped using it.

> I didn't apply the Association Test anymore, because it wasn't necessary. I learned what I had to learn from the exact examination of psychic reactions . . . You can demonstrate repression and the amnestic phenomena, the way people cover up . . . their emotions and so on. It is like an ordinary conversation, but seen and measured in principles. You observe all the things you observe in a conversation . . . little hesitations, mistakes in speech, certain gestures . . .
>
> (Jung 1957, p. 49)

Jung's early experimental research methods

In 1900, Freud's publication of 'On Dreams' began a scientific enquiry into depth psychology that continues today. Inspired by his work, C.G. Jung was starting his experimental researches as a young psychiatrist under the direction and guidance of Dr Eugene Bleuler at the Psychiatric Clinic of the University of Zurich (the Burgholzi). Having re-examined the experimental procedures of Wundt and Kraeplin and Riklin (CW 2), Jung applied methods of investigating the mental associations of patients with schizophrenia (then called 'dementia praecox') and other mental disorders. Jung and Riklin had agreed the concrete and modest goal: To use word association to help to differentiate between normal and abnormal subjects. Some 25 years later, Jung said that they had failed, as 'one can study nothing of the sort by such primitive means' (CW 18, para. 99).

But what he and Riklin had discovered was the value of 'mistakes' made by clients participating in the experiment.

> The interesting thing is why people could *not* react to certain stimulus words, or in entirely inadequate way.
>
> (Jung 1957, p. 11)

DOI: 10.4324/9781032716572-1

They came to regard these 'mistakes' as indicating disturbances resulting from complexes activated by the unconscious. Thus they became termed 'complex indicators'.

They include some of the defense mechanisms which had been observed by Freud, such as 'slips of the tongue', now popularly referred to as 'Freudian slips', or parapraxes.

A student once drew attention to an apparent example of a parapraxis, which she found in the McGuire and Hull (1973) edition of 'C.G. Jung speaking'. Here the reader is informed by the author that when talking about the AE, Jung stated that: 'We still use it in the training of young alienists' (p. 310). She felt perhaps that learning to make inferences from observations of unconscious phenomena seemed to the editor like discovering an alien language. Maybe this whole field of study felt somewhat 'alien'. But she also felt that it could also be that the AE helps readers to discover something valuable and transformative, which, by definition, is 'alien' until it is known. True as that might be, in fact, in this case the word 'alienist' is not a parapraxis. The term was used to decribe professionals working with mental illness before the term 'Psychiatrist' was introduced!

A probable parapraxis occurred in a training seminar in London, where a handout had been prepared by an author who had recently ended a relationship with the lecturer, a Freudian analyst. The happless presenter solemnly distributed the notes, in which, unnoticed in a paragraph deep in the text, it was stated that one should always carefully watch our for 'Freuedian shits'. (But perhaps the example was not altogether an unintentional slip of the tongue. One must be careful in making such observations).

The Association Experiment employed a combination of two approaches, word association and psycho-physical measurement. The word association part required the administration of a list of stimulus words and the measurement of the response times of the patient. Measurements were made with a stopwatch and were accurate to one-fifth of a second. At the same time, psychophysical measurements of muscle contraction and blood pressure were taken with a kymograph; electrical resistance across the skin was measured with a galvanometer and respiratory movement in the chest wall with a pneumograph.

Significantly, Jung found that the galvanic reaction depended on attention to the stimulus and the ability to 'associate it with other previous occurrences. This association may be conscious but is usually unconscious' (CW 2, para. 1311).

He also discovered that both the memory and anticipation evoked by a stimulus word created levels of response similar to those in a 'live' event.

The discovery of complexes

As is now apparent, Jung's 'experimental 'failures' were not the end but a beginning of a story, an inside account of which can be gleaned directly from his successive publications and interviews on the topic. These include *Studies in word association*; and *Psychophysical researches* (CW 2) and *On simulated insanity* (CW 1). His reflective views can be found in 'A Review of complex theory' (CW 8), The Tavistock lectures, 1936 (CW 18) and C. G. Jung, Richard Evans interviews (1957).

Through his word association experiments, Jung concluded that:

> In the depth of the mind of each hysterical patient we always find an old wound that still hurts or in psychological terms, a feeling toned complex.
>
> (CW 2, para. 915)

Of patients diagnosed with schizophrenia he wrote:

> In this too we are concerned with a complex buried in the depths of the mind . . .
>
> (CW 2, para. 916)

The discovery of the complex as a group of associated feeling-toned memories profoundly influenced depth psychology, and the related professions and the term 'complex' traveled speedily from professional vocabulary into common parlance (although Jung was keen to say that the full psychological meaning was not always fully grasped by the wider population).

> Everyone knows nowadays that people 'have complexes'. What is not so well known, though far more important theoretically, is that complexes can have us.
> (CW 8, para. 200)

What Jung meant by 'complex' can be best explained in his own words:

> Every constellation of a complex postulates a disturbed state of consciousness. The unity of consciousness is disrupted and the intentions of the will are impeded or made impossible. Even memory is often noticeably affected . . . an active complex puts us momentarily under a state of duress, of compulsive thinking and acting, for which under certain conditions the only appropriate term would be the judicial concept of diminished responsibility.
> (CW 8, para. 200)

We are often faced with the challenge of recognising patterns of feeling and behaviour which defy rationality. Reflecting on our lives, we can ask; 'What came over us? What were we thinking? Why do the same things keep happening to us, despite our best conscious efforts to avoid them?'

Working definitions

For the purposes of training candidates, we use the term 'Word Association Experiment' (WAE). We also prefer this term for use in general psychotherapy and consulting. The headline term 'experiment' is generally more conducive to the desired learning outcomes of the training than the word 'test', with its connotations of the client or patient 'being tested'.

However, when referring to the main body of empirical research, or to its use for diagnosing mental disorders, either directly or as an adjunct to other instruments, we use the term 'Word Association Test' (WAT).

These distinctions are based on a number of premises including the different objectives of the use of the instrument in different contexts considered against scientific definitions of 'experiment' and 'test' given by the American Psychological Association (2015) (see also glossary).

Familiarisation with precise classifications of usage and clear definitions is intended to help the practitioner to engage in multidisciplinary discourse and to avoid misuse.

Further to the glossary definitions, for quick reference, a short explanation of the WAT with illustrative quotes by C. G. Jung can be found at ARAS (Archive for Archetypal Research and Symbolism, https://aras.org/concordance/content/word-association-test).

Practical applications in training

It is our experience that the AE can yield measurable patient benefit, whether it is delivered separately or in combination with other 'psychological instruments'. It is best conducted in accordance with protocols based on post-Jungian and contemporary effectiveness research findings which emphasise the nature and quality of the therapist/patient relationship. Kast (1980) noted that it can assist therapeutic discussion and reflection at many points during the course of therapy and throughout a person's development.

Some analysts use it clinically as routine, some use it selectively and others, not at all. We use it selectively. Both the WAE and WAT have been used not only in therapeutic work but also in leadership and personal development in organisations and in forensic enquiries.

One of the main benefits of the training is sensitisation to complex indicators in self and others. It teaches observation, appreciative enquiry and analytic skills not only to candidates and psychoanalysts but also to professionals in related psychological disciplines.

For the practical training of candidates, we have taken into account the considerable developments in psychotherapy and research over the last 125 years, including recent Jungian research publications (for example; Roesler (2013, 2018) and the PAP-S-Rating-Manual (2014) published by the Swiss authorities). At the same time, we have attempted to convey the spirit and form of Jung's seminal work, giving references to the source material. Where we have made necessary adjustments to the seminal work, these are clearly noted and referenced.

If you aim to use this manual for training or for use with patients we ask you to proceed carefully. In conjunction with your reading it is necessary to familiarise yourself with the process by taking the experiment with a suitably qualified and trained analyst. It is usually the case that complexes can be triggered in the experimenter, and in some cases it is contra-indicated. Patient welfare is paramount, and professionalism demands that we only practice methods with which we are thoroughly conversant, preferably having experienced them ourselves and having practiced them under supervision.

Jung wrote:

... an inexperienced experimenter can make the gravest mistakes with this delicate material.
(CW 2, para. 761)

Practised with care, it can provide a robust training for analysts and 'alienists' alike, opening new dimensions of awareness, creativity and development for both patients and therapists.

References

American Psychological Association. 2015, *APA Dictionary of Psychology* (2nd ed.). <https://doi.org/10.1037/14646-000>.
ARAS. 2024, 'Word Association Test', *Archive for Archetypal Research and Symbolism*. Visited February 12, 2024. <https://aras.org/concordance/content/word-association-test>.
Jung, CG 1903, 'On simulated insanity', *Psychiatric Studies*, CW 1.
Jung, CG 1904–7/1910/1937, 'The psychological diagnosis of evidence', 'Psychophysical researches', *Experimental Researches*, CW 2.
Jung, CG 1910/1946, 'Psychic conflicts in a child', *The Development of Personality*, CW 17.
Jung, CG 1934, 'A review of complex theory', *The Structure and Dynamics of the Psyche*, CW 8.
Jung, CG 1935, 'Tavistock lectures', *The Symbolic Life*, CW 18.
Jung, CG 1957, C. G. Jung – Richard Evans Interviews Transcript of the 1957 Films.
Kast, V 1980, *Excerpts in English from 'Das assoziationsexperiment in der therapeutischen praxis'*, trans. Irene Gad, Bonz Verlag, Fellback-Oeffingen.
McGuire, W, Hull, RFC (eds.) 1973, *C. G. Jung Speaking, Interviews and Encounters*, Princeton University Press, Princeton.

Additional Resources

Evans, R, Kearnes, J 2020, *Conversations with Carl Jung and Reactions from Ernest Jones*, The University of Akron Press, Akron.
Freud, S 1909, 'Analysis of a phobia in a five-year old boy', *The Standard Edition of the Complete Psychological Works of Sigmund Freud*, SE, vol. 10, pp. 1–150.
Meier, CA 1994, *Die Empirie des Unbewussten. Mit besonderer Berücksichtigung des Assoziationsexperiment von C. G. Jung*, Daimon Verlag, Einsiedeln.

Roesler, C 2013, 'Evidence for the effectiveness of Jungian psychotherapy: A review of empirical studies', *Behavioural Sciences*, vol. 24, no. 3, pp. 562–575.
Roesler, C (ed.) 2018, *Research in Analytical Psychology: Empirical Research*, Routledge, London.
Thomas, D 1971, *Deaths and Entrances*, Dent, London.
Tschuschke, V, Koemeda-Lutz, M, Schlegel, M 2014, *PAP-S-Rating-Manual (PAP-S-RM): Rating Manual for the Objective Evaluation of Therapeutic Interventions of Psychotherapists Based on Various Theoretical Concepts*, Schriftenreihe der Schweizer Charta für Psychotherapie, Zurich.

2 WAE training for student analysts and practitioners

John O'Brien

Training rationale and overview

For students at a recognised training institute, registration for the WAE training and examinations are important steps which signify the training candidate's commitment to the rigours of the experiment itself and to further in-depth analytic study. The training is deep and thorough, and it is the gateway to becoming a candidate for the Diploma of the Institute, which involves further intensive periods of study, training, supervised practice, thesis writing and ongoing personal analysis.

The aim is to provide a safe and supportive guided learning environment in which candidates can successfully learn to conduct the WAE. In the introductory seminar, students are prepared for learning how to conduct the WAE under supervision and to give a report and presentation to peers and examiners.

Scientific framework

By the time students register for the WAE, they have already completed a substantial period of 'propadeuticum' study as a candidate for training, for which they have taken a range of examinations. The WAE training is therefore entered into with high mutual expectations of success. This positive framework both allows and encourages freedom to make non-critical mistakes and to learn safely, very much in the spirit of Jung's research which led to his theory of complexes. Patient well-being is the paramount consideration, and the experiment is controlled by a check on progress and final examination.

The training encourages both striving for excellence and acknowledgement of the inevitable mistakes and corrections which foster experiential learning, carefulness, self-awareness, curiosity, openness, and enjoyment of discovery. If the candidate develops these qualities wholeheartedly, then the patient can benefit as much from the developing character of the experimenter as from the experimental procedure.

It is sometimes imagined that psychotherapy can be practiced purely 'technically', as though it were a formula. The empirical aspects of the WAE make it vulnerable to such an approach, against which Jung strongly cautioned.

> It has long been imagined that psychotherapy can be practiced 'technically', as though it were a formula, a method of operation or a colour test . . . Psychotherapy cannot be used like that . . . the point is not the technique but the person who uses the technique.
>
> (CW 2, para. 337)

Function of the WAE as a 'rite of passage' in training

At the Carl Gustav Jung Institute in Zurich (CGJIZ) the WAE is a mandatory training, undertaken at the mid-point of the student's learning cycle. It is considered a 'rite of passage' which gives candidates access to new privileges and responsibilities (e.g. supervised clinical work, presentations, independent research and collegial relationships with practicing psychoanalysts, psychotherapists and psychiatrists.

The learning objectives incorporated into WAE training are therefore designed to foster the development of the knowledge, skills and attitudes necessary for students to achieve the Diploma and to work with patients, as well as to achieve a safe level of proficiency for future clinical practice.

Symbolic value of the WAE as a union of opposites

A less obvious and symbolic rationale for the timing of the WAE training can also be discerned by considering the WAE in the context of Jung's opus. Jung described psychological life in terms of individuation, a lifelong development process prompted by the tension and dialogue between the conscious and the unconscious. The WAE can be imagined as a bridge between these opposite dimensions of the psyche. In the same vein, it juxtaposes and connects the objective disciplines of scientific method and subjective processes. To some extent, it both relies upon the strengths and exposes the limitations of the traditional scientific method. It invites the practitioner into new realms of discovery, stimulating new perspectives from contemporary science which chime with Jung's work on symbols, synchronicity and the nature of the deep unconscious.

Developing the character of the analyst

The WAE offers much opportunity for the character development of the experimenter in preparation for their analytic work with patients and clients. The following quote from Jung, as with similar quotes in this manual, should be read non-gender specifically. The original translation has not been changed.

> Patients read the analyst's character intuitively, and they should find in him a man with failings, admittedly, but also a man who strives at every point to fulfill his human duties in the fullest sense.
>
> (CW 4, para. 587)

This explicit aim of the training finds a practical form in type psychology awareness. Although this is taught as a separate subject, many candidates bring their knowledge of type psychology learned in complimentary seminars into their word association training. Jung had noted that type psychology differences could be observed during the WAT.

Learning outcomes

To provide a fair and clear guide for candidates about which aspects of the WAE training are the focus of discussion, control and examination, we have provided a list of the desired learning outcomes (in what follows). It can be read in conjunction with the step-by-step learning guide given in the following chapter. The learning outcomes take into account both Jung's direct comments on the topic and key post-Jungian contemporary research into psychotherapeutic efficacy in general and the WAT in particular. (These topics are elaborated later in the manual.)

By the end of the training the student will be able to:

1. Appreciate the paramountcy of patient health and well-being in the WAE
2. Understand the origins and purposes of training in the WAE
3. Know the different uses and limitations of the WAE
4. Know where to look for contemporary empirical research on the WAE
5. Appreciate the research/practitioner value of the WAE
6. Understand limits, indications and cautions of use
7. Establish the boundary conditions for the experiment
8. Administer the experiment comfortably, using the template and a stopwatch while presenting stimulus words and observing and recording responses
9. Complete the supporting data analysis
10. Present the data according to the protocol
11. Form an initial hypothesis
12. Deliver the context interview, inviting further associations, elaborations and clarifications noting feelings, images, contents and the client's chains of associations and connections
13. Identify field phenomena
14. Identify complexes apparent during the WAE
15. Form a draft map of complexes with an appropriate level of patient involvement
16. Identify archetypes and symbols of transformation
17. Facilitate patient reflection and implications for therapy
18. Record personal learning
19. Give a presentation
20. Be familiar with modern delivery methods (e.g. Zoom)

Additional Resources

Jung, CG 1904–7/1910, 'Studies in word association', *Experimental Researches*, CW 2.
Jung, CG 1906/1949, *Freud and Psychoanalysis*, CW 4.

3 Preparing for the AE

John O'Brien

Step-by-step learning guide

1 **Read.** Preparation usually begins by reading about Jung's early experimental researches with the Word Association Experiment/Word Association Test. (References are provided in Chapter 1.) Preliminary areas of concern or special interest can be discussed with an analyst. As there will be limited time during the seminar training for Q&A it is best to formulate remaining questions in advance so that helpful discussions can take place and useful answers may be given.

2 **Take the AE yourself.** We recommend that the experimenter takes the AE with a qualified analyst who is experienced in conducting the experiment. It is essential to have experienced the experiment yourself and have practiced it before conducting the first experiment with a client or patient. It is important to take the AE in a language in which you are comfortable, and training seminars and templates are available in different languages. If you are multilingual, it is advisable to choose the language in which you are most fluent, use most regularly, and in which you dream.

3 **Sign up.** Register for the introductory training seminar.

4 **Sign up again.** Register for the examination. It is not mandatory to take the examination with the same lecturers who have delivered the introductory seminar, but you should check it with the chosen examiner. Check the examination dates as well as seminar training slots to make sure that you have a comfortable preparation schedule, and sign up accordingly. It is important that you let the chosen examiner know that you have registered for the exam so that you can receive the deadlines for different requirements of the process. Administrative details vary between Institutes and training organisations. You are free to choose examination dates and examiners as available. We recommend that you do this at least five months in advance to give yourself time to prepare, conduct and write up the WAE (see what follows).

5 **Inform your analyst.** The training is designed to increase awareness of your complexes and type psychology, and learning can be greatly accelerated by sharing whatever you feel is appropriate with your analyst. Letting them know in advance will help them to help you with your own complexes triggered during the experiment.

6 **Attend AE seminar 1: Introduction to the Association Experiment.** The seminar may be conducted in vivo or online. The main points in this manual are covered in the seminar, and questions are encouraged. The aims of the seminar are to establish a comfortable learning environment and to make sure that you are familiar with the process and that you know how and where to find support (from tutors or peers) when needed.

7 **Select a patient or client.** It is recommended that you select a person of whom you have no personal knowledge, existing clients or patients excepted, and where there are no

DOI: 10.4324/9781032716572-3

contra-indications for them undertaking the experiment. It is advised not to conduct the experiment with relatives, partners, friends or fellow candidates you know well.

8. **Establish the frame.** The frame includes the content and manner in which the experiment is first described to the client/patient, usually at least two weeks before the experiment takes place. The introductory letter and subsequent letters have been carefully worded, and it is advisable to provide them both verbally and in writing at the appropriate point in the process.

9. **Check or conduct the anamnesis.** Instructions for conducting the anamnesis are given in Chapter 4. If you are working with an existing client or patient and already have an anamnesis, check it against the structure given in Chapter 4. There are many forms of anamnesis. The one given here includes developmental and psycho-social factors including birth order characteristics. These provide useful triangulation points when forming a hypothesis after the context interview. If you need to backfill missing sections from the anamnesis, then this can be done later with material from the context interview.

10. **Practice without a patient or client.** It can at first be a little awkward reading the stimulus words, observing reactions, recording complex indicators and using a stopwatch all at the same time. It is best to take some time to practice with a friend or fellow candidate, using a few neutral stimulus words only, until you can present the words in an even tone and in a comfortable rhythm.

11. **Conduct part 1 of the experiment**. When you are prepared, proceed with conducting the experiment as described in Chapter 5.

12. **Complete the 'offline' analysis.** This is explained in Chapter 5. Again, if extra help is required at this stage, communicate with examiner by email. Refer also to the example given in Chapter 5.

13. **Prepare for and conduct part 2 of the experiment, the context interview.** This is explained in Chapter 6.

14. **Read.** Familiarise yourself with the final exam document structure.

15. **Mid-point Check.** Send the completed template with the analysis of the protocol to the examiner with any questions. The examiner will reply with comments and further guidance.

16. **Complete the interpretation hypothesis and your version of the complex map.** This is described in Chapter 7.

17. **Send the first draft of the completed AE document to the examiner**. The examiner will study it and reply with further guidance (either accept the document or ask for some edits).

18. **Discuss the process with the client or patient.** In the example version of the AE, the complex map and implications are fully discussed with the patient. The level of client participation can vary from passive participation to full active participation in the interpretation and construction of meaning. The relevance of this is explained in Chapter 8. Your choice of method will depend upon your professional experience, comfort with the process and the client–analyst relationship.

19. **Prepare and present.** Write up and deliver the experiment to peers and tutors at examination.

Uses of the AE

There are many uses for the WAE. In this manual, we have focused on its use as a safe vehicle for the teaching and learning of Jungian psychoanalytic and psychotherapeutic knowledge, skills and attitudes. This demands adherence to the protocol and compliance with the codes of ethics and standards of professional conduct of the institution or training organisation overseeing the training. The training methods are subject to update and review. They are published in this manual and in forthcoming revisions.

The WAE or its derivatives may be used for the identification of complexes as defined by C. G. Jung and elaborated in this volume.

In the light of post-Jungian and contemporary research, each part of the WAE has been carefully reconsidered for inclusion in the template. All parts of the template must be completed and considered together to demonstrate the triangulation of evidence required for the identification of complexes.

The WAE may be used to help patients or clients to develop new conscious perspectives on thoughts, feelings and behaviour patterns, from which viewpoints unconscious, autonomous characteristics of complexes may be modified.

It may be used specifically to help the patient to differentiate the ego complex from parental and other complexes.

Where the AE/WAE has been used either as a stand-alone or in conjunction with other psychological tests, it may be used in accordance with the established research for the stated purposes and within the limits of professional competence of the practitioner.

It may be used repeatedly at different stages of therapy to promote individuation.

In all usages, training or otherwise, client or patient well-being is paramount.

Misuse

We advise against the use of the WAE for purposes other than those which are supported by evidence-based research and/or which fall outside the defined professional limits of the practitioner.

Kast emphasised caution when considering the use of the WAE with patients/clients with impaired major ego functioning and low ego strength. These are defined psychoanalytically by Blackman (2023) as abstraction, integration and reality testing; and impulse control, affect tolerance and containing primary processes. We also caution against using the WAE in situations in which patients have been recently traumatised (for example through bereavement) or are suffering psychotic symptoms.

Research ethics protocol

If you are conducting the experiment as part of an additional research protocol, make sure that you adhere fully to the protocol and are compliant with the ethics.

Letter of introduction example

Below is provided a 'strawman' guidance note introducing a client or patient to the Word Association Experiment a few weeks before conducting the experiment. We advise that you construct your own introduction well in advance. It can be tailored to your own professional context and, ideally, to the client or patient's particular expectations and concerns.

> The Word Association Experiment (WAE) is an exploration, based on Carl Jung's work. It has been scientifically retested and developed for more than 125 years.
>
> It is completely confidential. (As I am in training) I will share the anonymised results with my training analyst and in my supervision and examination. None of your personal details will be shared. I will check with you at each step of the process to make sure that

you are comfortable with this arrangement. I am bound by the professional code of ethics of my institute and my agency.

The WAE, which is also known as the Word Association Test, goes back to the beginning of the 20th century when Jung, together with colleagues and students, began his experimentation with word association at the Psychiatric Clinic of the University of Zurich.

We now think of it as an experiment, as this indicates that there is no 'pass' or 'fail', and that all answers are legitimate and useful in the process of discovery.

The experiment starts with a list of carefully chosen 50 (or 100) stimulus words, based on Jung's research, which are presented one by one. You are asked to respond by simply saying the first word which comes to mind. People respond to the words differently, according to their own associations. There are no right answers. All answers help us to identify possible complexes. Jung's definition of a complex is an unconscious, organised set of feeling-toned memories, organised around strong emotions. (The American Psychological Association Dictionary defines complexes as 'a group or system of related ideas or impulses that have a common emotional tone and exert a strong but usually unconscious influence on the individual's attitudes and behaviour').

The WAE gives a snapshot of complexes constellated in the psyche in a particular context at a particular point in time. It can also give pointers to long standing complexes likely to appear in the future.

Becoming conscious of complexes, regardless of whether they point to possible traumas or moments of great pleasure, is an important step in getting to know more about yourself and how perception, decisions and actions can be affected without one's awareness.

About the WAE process

The Word Association Experiment is conducted over a minimum of three separate meetings.

Usually, the process begins with an opportunity for you to share your **personal history**. This takes between one hour and 90 minutes. Next, administering the experiment with the word list and responses takes around one hour. After a week or so, when I have reviewed the results, we have a further (context) discussion (60–90 minutes) about the findings. It will provide an opportunity for us to share and compare insights.

This can be followed up by one or two sessions further exploring how the insights reveal 'complexes'.

It is useful for these sessions to be scheduled within a two- or three-week period, so that not too much time passes by between the three meetings: Personal history, WAE administration and the context discussion.

Using the results

You own the results. All information is treated with full confidentiality and in accordance with my professional ethics and the laws governing the handling of client information.

Structure of the AE final exam document

1 Anamnesis
2 Description of the experimental setting and initial counter-transference
3 Analysis of the feedback after the first part of the experiment and Data from the Unconscious

4 Analysis of Protocol

   a Tables and graphs
   b Prolonged response times
   c Analysis by complex indicators
   d Qualitative analysis of responses
   e Response reactions and thoughts about perseveration

5 Context interview
6 Interpretation hypothesis

   a Map of complexes
   b Synopsis of the main findings

7 Indications for further therapeutic work
8 Reflections on the AE experience for the candidate's individuation process
9 Candidate's own complexes evoked during the AE

4 Taking the anamnesis

John O'Brien

Introduction

Before conducting the Word Association Experiment, it is usual to take an account of the patient's personal history in the form of an anamnesis. This is not simply a case history which draws upon information and types of data drawn from medical and/or bio-psycho-social test records but also a record of client recollections and remembrances, both personal and collective (e.g. family stories), from the client's point of view. It includes the patient's narrative.

In clinical practice it often follows the preliminary stages of an intake procedure or 'chemistry check', in which both parties take the first steps towards building a therapeutic working alliance. (Questions are asked such as 'what brings you here?' and 'What would you like to see as a result of therapy?').

Guidance

During training it is not required to identify unconscious material during the course of the anamnesis. At this point it suffices to work on the simple assumption that 'the conscious content from which our work starts is the anamnesis' (CW 4, para. 528).

That said, reflection might inform us that during the anamnesis, conscious material is gathered from which symbolic meaning later becomes apparent. Jung gives the example of an account of a patient's mountain sickness given in an anamnesis (CW 16, para. 303) as a symbolic representation (confirmed subsequently by a dream to the same effect) of his/her inability to 'climb any further' (CW 16, para. 303).

The task then is to help the client to feel safe and comfortable enough to give their personal story in a semi-structured format.

This is achieved by providing a clear framework supported by a therapeutic attitude and qualities which accord with research findings of common human factors which promote positive therapeutic outcomes. These include, for example: (a) personal analyst qualities of warmth, genuineness, empathy, respect; (b) behaviors including active listening, summary and reflection; and an attitude of curiosity and 'not knowing'. An anamnesis built on such foundations then includes gentle questioning, prompting of recollection and the recording of data.

We might consider the anamnesis as an experiment, a mutual step into the unknown. As such it is not merely a fact-gathering exercise. It draws upon our type psychology and capacities for analytic holding, listening and appreciative enquiry.

> We begin with the anamnesis, as is customary in medicine in general and psychiatry in particular – that is to say, we try to piece together the historical facts of the case as

flawlessly as possible. The psychotherapist, however, does not rest content with these facts . . . At all events one must be prepared not to hear the very things that are most important . . . he has to rely on intuitions and sudden ideas, and the more widely he casts his net of questions, the more likely he is to succeed in catching the complex nature of the case . . . His assessment of anamnesis data may be very different from a purely medical one.

(CW 16, para. 194)

Aims

In the context of the AE, the aims of the anamnesis are:

1 To take a first step in therapeutic enquiry
2 To gather information on 'conscious contents' from the client's perspective
3 To build trust and rapport in support of a working alliance
4 To stimulate client reflection
5 To establish a safe platform and climate for conducting the AE protocol
6 To start to notice 'unconscious contents'
7 To create a relational climate in which unconscious material can be safely explored during the AE

Practical guide

The anamnesis is taken in a secure and comfortable environment, with no interruptions and with confidentiality guaranteed. The anamnesis can be taken face to face or online. For training purposes we recommend face-to-face work. It can be helpful to record the meeting and produce a transcript, but client preferences and confidentiality should be taken into account.

Example introduction

> We usually take a personal history to help you to prepare for the Association Experiment. We call this an anamnesis because it is your own account of what you remember (or have been told) about events which seem significant to you rather than simply objective records. The AE is an experiment to help you to discover more about yourself, and the anamnesis is a first step in this process. We can start either with early memories and work forwards or with recent memories and work backwards. Either approach is fine, and I will help you by asking a few questions as we go along.
>
> It is a confidential exercise conducted under the auspices of (for example, the CG Jung Institute, where I am a candidate for training). I subscribe to the Code of Ethics of the Institute and the State laws regarding the handling of personal information. Your private and personal details will be treated confidentially. I propose to share the data from the anamnesis experiment anonymously with examiners and colleagues as part of my training. I will check with you after the experiment to ask your permission to use the data in this way.

The anamnesis is usually given in a series of short narrative statements and associations made by the client, and elaboration can be encouraged by the analyst by summary, reflection, prompts and open-ended questioning. The anamnesis is just a first step, and it can be helpful to the client to be steered in a gentle and friendly manner so that a representative span of important recollections is covered within 1 to 1.5 hours and can be represented in the AE document in a page or two.

Following are some headings which can be used to guide the session in a semi-structured format:

1. Presenting problem
2. Expectations about the AE
3. Stories or knowledge about birth circumstances and early childhood
4. Place in birth order (siblings), parents and carers
5. Ancestors
6. Early social context and climate (for example, born in a period of war)
7. Education
8. Economic circumstances
9. Occupational situation
10. Interests
11. Present family and circumstances
12. Significant others
13. Significant events
14. Significant problems
15. Pervasive themes

In clinical practice it is not uncommon for the anamnesis to begin with a problem statement, or 'presenting problem'. It can be accompanied by the reason for referral. This is the client's view of why they are here at this moment. It can naturally lead to an expression of hopes and doubts about potential outcomes.

The anamnesis is not intended to be exhaustive (or exhausting!). It can also be helpful to note what is not covered and to see if this is forthcoming in the 'context discussion'. The information given might, for various reasons, change during the course of the anamnesis or afterwards.

Example anamnesis

The example is a fictitious composite of cases drawn from a range of sources over 10 years.

Client Identifying code: D 4483
Gender identity: Female
Age: 44 (born 1972)

Parents and carers

D's mother was born in 1952 in a poor part of Europe, the younger of two sisters by three years. She committed suicide when D was an adult.

D's father was born in 1944. He had a son from his first marriage. D was the only child of his third marriage. He worked as a solicitor.

Position in birth order (when there are siblings)

D has a half-brother who is 11 years older than her. They had a close relationship.

Ancestors

D's maternal grandmother (MGM) did not provide adequate food and clothing for D's mother.

D spoke with affection about her paternal grandmother (PGM), who she described as a kind woman.

D did not speak about her paternal grandparents.

Stories or knowledge about birth circumstances and early childhood

Although she reports no complications with her birth, her mother found it impossible to breast feed her. She suffered from depression. On reflection, D feels that she had been a burden on her mother.

Childhood and youth

D's earliest memories are of walks with her mother to bookstores and shops, but the mother never wanted to buy anything for D. D wore clothes of other children in the family. D remembers her father as always very strict, she never knew in what mood he would be. He always shouted. Her first memory of him was him bringing home a little fox he found while hunting. She loved animals from her early childhood to date. D was quite sick as a child (chicken pox, pneumonia), and she remembers her father reading to her. He was rarely warm, but it felt nice when he was. D remembers that her parents quarreled a lot throughout her childhood.

Due to her parents' constant quarrels, when D was 12, she went to an institution for children without parental care on her own and asked to be admitted. She was not admitted, and her parents divorced soon after. D's half brother and her father also quarreled a lot, and quarrels are the most present theme in her childhood. When the father forbade her brother to study movie production (what he really wanted) the brother started drinking and remained alcoholic for the rest of his life. D remembers her half-brother as rebellious, always saying openly what he meant, down to earth. Both father and brother loved animals, but her mother did not like them. Both mother and father constantly compared her with other children from their sides of the family, and they were always better than her in everything. (After her mother left, she terminated any contact with wider family members.)

When D was about to finish high school, her mother arranged for her to go to teacher training college, and her father entered her for law school. D ran away from home and enrolled in veterinary science. Nothing she or her brother did was good enough for her father. When D was 18 her mother left to live in Germany, and at that moment D bought her first dog. Since then, she has always had animals. After a few years she decided to marry her boyfriend but then ran away from her own wedding – to Germany. By that time, her mother was very ill with rheumatism and had suffered 11 surgeries. D worked as an air hostess stewardess, traveling a lot.

Social context and climate (for example, born in a period of war)

D was born in a middle-low-income country in a climate of social conflict. She migrated to West European country when she was 18, and when she was in her 20s, war broke out. Her brother fought in the war and suffered undiagnosed severe PTSD. She managed her life to make it possible for him to visit her for long periods of convalescence.

Education

D is a highly educated person, well-read, very curious about different topics. She has a post-graduate university degree in photography and related subjects.

Economic circumstances

D had been working as a stewardess while supporting herself and her sick mother. At 39 years old D was diagnosed with breast cancer. She had to stop working while going through her medical treatment. D then returned to her home country and struggled to find a steady job. D did not seem to be very rational with managing her finances and left an impression of always struggling financially.

Occupations and interests

D worked as a stewardess, then as a project manager in an large organisation embassy, and at present she is a project manager in an organisation supporting children. She has been engaged with dogs (exhibitions, breeding, care) all her life. She enjoys making photographic and film documentaries.

Significant events

While D was employed as a stewardess, she worked three shifts, supporting both herself and her mother and two friends who ran away from her native country, which at that time was in a state of war. D visited her father who got ill, and he soon died.

She fell in love with a person whom her mother did not trust. She kept saying he wanted to marry D because of her status in Germany. Eventually, her mother's views proved to be correct, and he soon left D. A few years later she met an Englishman whom she loved most in her life and had a great time together for 2 years. He had a girlfriend in England, was honest about that, and they kept spending weekends together traveling to different places. At one point D realised that she loved him so much that she could not continue unless the relationship was exclusive, and she decided not to see him ever again. Since then she did not have a serious relationship.

A few years after, D's best friend, who was visiting, found D's mother dead. She had committed suicide by hanging. D returned to her native country, lived as a sub-tenant and sold nuts on the market to survive. A year after that D's brother died of a stroke. That is when she found a job as a project manager.

Present family and circumstances

Four years ago D had breast cancer diagnosed and went through difficult surgery and tough treatment. She is now the project manager of an international organisation caring for children with challenging backgrounds and is finishing her studies (film production). She is making documentaries and enjoys it a great deal. She is still under a heavy hormonal therapy and has put on a lot of weight due to the treatment, and she is bothered about it. D has two dogs and a cat, and her dog has been winning trophies at the exhibitions till recently, when D decided to stop doing this and let her dog be just playful. D does not have children. She said that she did get pregnant with the first boyfriend. Her mother had said that D will have her baby 'over her dead body'.

Significant problems

Except for her illness, D herself did not report any significant problems. She mentioned only that sometimes she gets very angry and that sometimes she feels very sad and lonely. At the outset, I had the initial thought of a borderline disorder.

Pervasive themes

Quarrels, conflicts, extreme situations, apparently opposite topics 'see-saw' (such as very spiritual topics and then primal dramas like exploration of dog fights), always something marked with drama.

Expectations about the AE

D was very excited about going through the AE process, and she was very curious about the experiment. She said that she was hopeful that it might bring her peace.

Special characteristics of the Jungian anamnesis

The anamnesis in a Jungian context has special characteristics. It is not necessary to be familiar with these for the examination; they are included here for those with a deeper interest in this specific topic. They can be most simply explained with reference to the dictionary.

Anamnesis is firstly defined as a recollection of past events, or the case history of a patient. As demonstrated in the example, the version we have given is more of a psycho-social reflection than a case history. We have also noted the importance of the therapeutic attitude of the analyst. This accords with Jung's guidance on the topic.

> We begin with the anamnesis, as is customary in medicine in general and psychiatry in particular – that is to say, we try to piece together the historical facts of the case as flawlessly as possible. The psychotherapist, however, does not rest content with these facts . . . At all events one must be prepared not to hear the very things that are most important . . . he has to rely on intuitions and sudden ideas, and the more widely he casts his net of questions, the more likely he is to succeed in catching the complex nature of the case . . . His assessment of anamnesis data may be very different from a purely medical one.
> (CW 16, para. 194)

Secondly, the expanded definition of anamnesis (Collins, 2024) has additional inclusions surprisingly relevant to Jungian work.

1. Reminiscence: The recollection or remembrance of the past.
2. In Platonism: recollection of the Ideas, which the soul had known in a previous existence, esp. by means of reasoning.
3. Diagnostics: The medical history of a patient.
4. In immunology: a prompt immune response to a previously encountered antigen, characterised by more rapid onset and greater effectiveness of antibody and T cell reaction than during the first encounter, as after a booster shot in a previously immunised person.
5. In the Christian Church: a prayer in a Eucharistic service, recalling the Passion, Resurrection, and Ascension of Christ.

The additional definitions, 2, 4 and 5 invite consideration of Jung's deeper perspectives on the process.

> Platonism: A good account of Plato's exposition of anamnesis and its significance for different religions is given in the *Encyclopedia of Religion* (2023). A further account is provided by Aronson (2020) from the Centre for Evidence Based Medicine in Oxford's Nuffield Department of Primary Care Health Sciences.
> Immunology: The prompt immune response also seems an appropriate analogy describing the therapeutic psychological mechanism of the anamnesis and psychotherapy in general.
> Christianity: The Christian reference is well explained by Schmidt (2023) with reference to Smolarski (1990) as follows:

Christian worship is fundamentally anamnestic, as an act in which 'the present is brought into intimate contact with the past' and vice-versa. However, this description of anamnesis is more akin to actualizing remembrance than merely active remembrance.

A peculiarly Jungian aspect of the anamnesis is that the process deeply resembles the psychotherapy per se, as does the WAE. This fact attracted criticism that Jungian psychotherapy was merely an extended anamnesis. This overlooked an appreciation that a deeper connecting theme was expressing itself recursively through Jung's opus, that the parts were also images of the whole while also needing to be differentiated from it. It is not certain that Jung himself was aware of this. In response to criticism, Jung replied with the following differentiating statement:

> The psychoanalyst naturally makes his anamnesis as carefully as any other specialist. But this is merely the patient's history and must not be confused with analysis.
>
> (CW 4, para. 525)

On the conscious and unconscious aspects of the anamnesis, he added:

> In contradistinction to all previous methods, psychoanalysis endeavours to overcome the disorders of the neurotic psyche through the unconscious, and not from the conscious side. In this work we naturally have need of the patient's conscious contents, for only in this way can we reach the unconscious. The conscious content from which our work starts is the material supplied by the anamnesis.
>
> (CW 4, para. 528)

Finally, the value of co-constructing and/or sharing the anamnesis with the client or patient is made evident in Jung's comment that:

> In many cases the anamnesis provides useful clues which make the psychic origin of his symptoms clear to the patient. This, of course, is necessary only when he is convinced that his neurosis is organic in origin. But even in those cases where the patient is convinced from the start of the psychic nature of his illness, a critical survey of the anamnesis can be of advantage, for it discloses a psychological context of which he was unaware before.
>
> (CW 4, para. 528)

If not during the anamnesis itself, during such reflections it is sometimes possible to take account of trans-generational phenomena.

References

Aronson, J 2020, 'When I use a word anamnesis'. Visited February 12, 2024. <https://blogs.bmj.com/bmj/2020/02/21/jeffrey-aronson-when-i-use-a-word-anamnesis>.
Collins Dictionary 2024. Available from: www.collinsdictionary.com [Accessed 01.10.2024]
Jung, CG 1909/1949, *Freud and Psychoanalysis*, CW 4.
Jung, CG 1931/1951, *The Practice of Psychotherapy*, CW 16.
Schmidt, W 2023, 'A theological, historical and social study of Anamnesis in Christian liturgy'. Visited February 13, 2024, <https://catholiccanada.wordpress.com/2012/04/23/a-theological-historical-and-social-study-of-anamnesis-in-christian-liturgy>.
Smolarski, D 1990, *Liturgical Literacy: From Anamnesis to Worship*, Paulist Press, New York.

5 AE protocol

John O'Brien

Example of a completed AE template

Here is a completed 50-word template. It records and categorises reactions to stimulus words. The template is followed by an explanatory table.

No.	SW	1/5	RT	RW	Rep	PRT	CI Code	CIT	Obj	E/c
1	play	9	1,7	alley	s					√
2	mouth	9	1,9	word	s				√	
3	free	49	9,8	happiness	open sea	T	S (P)	3		√
4	car	18	3,6	end	s		(p)			√
5	make	9	1,7	chaos	shit			1		√
6	friend	9	1,8	V	s			1		√
7	stupid	19	1,9	happy	fool		S	2		√
8	together	14	2,7	sharing	s			1		√
9	go	30	5,9	far	s	T		2		√
10	habit	49	9,7	monotony	boredom	T	(P)	2		√
11	new	18	3,6	challenge	experience		St, S,(p)	3		√
12	tree	12	2,3	stalk	s		(p)		√	
13	kiss	16	3,1	slap	s		MW, B, l	3		√
14	finger	7	1,4	direction	s					√
15	sad	22	4,4	unaware	alone	T	B (P)	3		√
16	knife	19	3,7	pain	anatomy	T		2		√
17	dance	18	3,5	hall	s				√	
18	choice	16	3,2	problem	bravery		St, S	3		√
19	naked	34	6,8	happy	free	T	St, S	4		√
20	plain	12	2,4	clever	cheek			1		√
21	learn	19	3,8	freedom	richness	T	st	3		√
22	pity	14	2,7	stupidity	s		St, S	2		√
23	weak	19	3,7	ignorant	not stupid	T	B, MW, st, S	6		√
24	boss	39	7,8	anarchy	s	T		1		√
25	wait	16	3,2	hope	losing time		MW	2		√
26	family	28	5,6	beehive	voice	T	B, st	3		√
27	sick	55	11	brave	alone	T	S (P)	3		√
28	cat	22	4,3	play	s	T	B	2		√
29	pray	30	5,9	desperate	weakness	T	(p)	3		√
30	wages	17	3,4	merit	s		st	1		√

(Continued)

DOI: 10.4324/9781032716572-5

(Continued)

No.	SW	1/5	RT	RW	Rep	PRT	CI Code	CIT	Obj	E/c
31	old	17	3,3	quality	experience		St, S	3		√
32	fight	33	6,5	bravery	Titans	T	S	3		√
33	glass	22	4,4	bottom	s	T	B, l, MW	4		√
34	marry	98	19,5	cage	don't know	T	(P)	2		√
35	guilt	25	4,9	mistake	s	T	(p)	1		√
36	work	17	3,4	must	obligation		st	2		√
37	proud	24	4,7	brave	s	T	St, S (P)	3		√
38	fear	18	3,5	stupidity	flying		S (p)	2		√
39	red	17	3,3	black	s		(p)		√	
40	water	12	2,4	depth	Open sea		B, MW, st	3		√
41	hurt	23	4,6	selfish	stupid	T	MW, S	4		√
42	flower	35	7,1	hippie sign	s	T	(P)	1		√
43	evil	22	4,3	anger	man		B, MW (p)	3		√
44	party	31	6,1	boredom	s	T		1		√
45	fly	12	2,4	fear	s	T		1		√
46	death	17	3,3	inevitability	s					√
47	clean	23	4,6	FALSE	problem			1		√
48	try	17	3,4	know	brave	T	MW, st, S	5		√
49	sin	21	4,1	experience	s		St, S	2		√
50	home	18	3,5	tweed	s	T		1		√

Explanation of the template: Column headings and definitions

No.	Reference number for the Stimulus Word
SW	Stimulus Word
1/5	Reaction time in fifths of a second, rounded off to nearest whole number
RT	Reaction time digitally recorded
RW	Reaction Word given in first round
Rep	Reaction Word given in second round
PRT	Prolonged reaction time
CI Code	Code for the complex indicator (see table that follows)
CIT	Sum of complex indicators horizontally in (columns 6, 7 & 8)
Obj	Factual (Objective) response The original term 'Factual' was used.
Ego/c	Egocentric (Subjective response)

Complex indicator codes and definitions

These are used when conducting the experiment and are entered as appropriate in the CI Column.

B	**Bodily movement mimic or laughter**. Any bodily movement, such as hand or head movements, may be additionally noted.
DR	**Disconnected reaction**. Appears meaningless but actually refers to an object or idea not connected to the stimulus word, for example a coffee cup on the client's desk.
F	**No verbal response within 30 seconds**. The original term 'failed reaction' was used.

(Continued)

(Continued)

Fl	**Foreign language reaction**, not in common use.
M	**Meaningless reaction.** Usually sounds, e.g. 'burble garble'. Although no response is meaningless, this does not convey immediate and commonly intelligible information.
Med	**Mediate reaction.** The first reaction is fully or partially suppressed and replaced with another word.
MSW	**Multiple word response.** Many words often including chains of associations, sentences and questions.
Ne	**Neologism, colloquialism, strong language**.
PRT	**Prolonged Reaction Time.** [1] Reaction time above the median. For the median Jung's used the term the 'probable mean'.
Px	**Paraprax** Slip of the tongue
Re	**Different or no reproduction word given in the second round.** Jung used the term 'false' reaction.
RSW	**Repetition of the stimulus word.** This includes repetition with rising intonation, for example 'play?'
S	**Stereotype.** Same reaction word used on 3 or more occasions in first and second run combined.
So	**Clang, rhyme or quotation.** Clangs are sound associations, such as 'clang-bang'. They are specific rhymes where the association is onomatopoeic.
St	**Stuttering or mispronunciation.**

Note: **(P)** and **(p)** indicate perseverations. **(P)** indicates the initial elevated response and **(p)** the subsequently affected words. This typically produces a 'downward staircase' effect in the bar graph. Perseverations are noted in the CI column but not counted as complex indicators. They are therefore marked in brackets to differentiate them.

How to administer the AE using the template

The WAT template is administered in two separate meetings, the administration meeting and the context interview. During the first meeting, the WAT template is administered in two 'runs', and during meeting the context discussion is conducted.

In this chapter we cover only the first meeting. Enough time (around one week) should be allowed between the two meetings to allow for charts and tables to be completed comfortably and for reflection before the second meeting.

First 'administration' meeting

The first meeting is divided into to two separate 'runs' (or 'trials').

At the start of the first run, we usually begin with an introduction:

> I will read to you 50 words, one after the other. To each of these words you are requested to answer, as quickly as possible, with the very first word, thing that occurs to you in connection to that word. Please answer with one word only. I will measure the time you take to answer. It is important that you say the very first word that comes to your mind.

(Kast 1980, p. 10)

Once you have used the WAT this way several times, you might experiment with recording AE or WAT sessions on Zoom, in which circumstance we recommend an additional communication as follows:

> Usually, I make a note of your response times and write them down during the experiment, but a recording allows me to do this more precisely. This makes it easier for me to concentrate on what you are saying. A recording also helps me to notice things which I might miss during the session. I will also send you a transcript of the session, which I will do once we have completed both meetings. The recording is confidential information and subject to the laws of the country or state concerning freedom of information and managed in accordance with the guidelines of my professional body and my practice.

In order to ensure that the instructions are understood, it can be useful to do a 'dry run' with some 'harmless' words. It is not always possible to be sure that a given word is indeed harmless to a given client, and Kast suggests using words such as 'tree', 'wood' or 'running'. If, during the dry run, the client reacts with more than one word, they are reminded to answer with only one word. If multiple-word responses continue, they are not corrected but regarded as symptomatic and noted on the template as a multiple-word response as complex indicator (MW).

The experimenter proceeds to calmly and clearly enunciate the Stimulus Word (SW) and begins to measure the reaction time between the presentation of the stimulus word and hearing the reaction word. As it takes approximately one-fifth of a second to actually pronounce a word with one syllable and two-fifths of a second to pronounce a word with two syllables, for practical purposes, this instruction is accurate enough. Alternatively, the experimenter may start measuring when the 'first vowel of the first accentuated syllable (of the stimulus word) is pronounced' and stop measuring 'at the first audible letter of the reaction word spoken by the client' (Kast 1980, p. 10). Nowadays, the reaction time is measured digitally, correct to one (or two) decimal place(s) and entered into the RT column. This is simply because most recording instruments measure in decimals. It is later converted to 1/5 of a second and noted on the template in the 1/5 column next to the Stimulus Word. This is because Jung found more precise measurement both impractical and not scientifically relevant. If the reaction time is longer than 30 seconds, it is recorded as 'no response' (F).

During the experiment, in the first run the experimenter fills in only the three columns marked in bold in the table that follows.

No.	SW	1/5	RT	RW	Rep	PRT	CI Code	CIT	Obj	Ego/c
33	glass		4,4	bottom			b, l, MW			

To recap, the process for the first run is:

1 Present the Stimulus Word.
2 Note the reaction time (digitally to one or two decimal places) and enter it in the RT column.
3 Note complex indicators and enter them in the CI column using the codes given in the above table.

For training purposes we recommend manual data entry on a printed copy of the template. Many experimenters report that during their first experiments, this is easier than entering observations directly onto the digital template. After practice, direct input onto a digital template is the preferred approach. A stopwatch (digital) is used to record the times. (As experimenters become proficient, and for certain purposes, there are a number of advantages to using video recordings and transcripts for more precise observation and feedback and a manual stopwatch is rarely used. These are discussed later in the manual.)

Once the first run has been completed, a short break of 15 minutes or so is given. The second run begins with the following instructions:

> We will repeat the experiment in order to ascertain what you remember. The time will not be measured now. If you do not remember the word you said the first time around, it is OK to just say a new word if one occurs to you.

The process for the second run is then simply to re-present the stimulus words and note the reactions in the Reproduction Column (Rep). If the reproduction word is the same as the SW, simply mark the box with an 's'. Do not leave the box blank, as doing so makes it difficult to check errors of omission later.

After both runs of the experiment have been completed, time should be taken to discuss the person's experience of the test. We concur with Kast (1980) that this discussion is useful because it also can show the experimenter when the client has observed that a complex has been constellated or provide clarification on points where they had difficulty in associating. Such difficulties might indicate that a complex is pressing. Jung gave specific guidance on establishing, after the experiment, whether or not a response was unconscious.

In response to a question about the unconscious (posed by Dr Eric B. Strauss during the Tavistock Lectures in September 1935), Jung replied:

> How can you establish whether the thing is conscious or unconscious? You simply ask people. We have no other criterion to establish whether something is conscious or unconsciousness. You say "Do you know that you had certain hesitations?" They say, "No I had no hesitation; to my knowledge I had the same reaction time". "Are you conscious that something disturbed you?" "No I am not." "Have you no recollection of what you answered to the word knife?" "None at all". "This unawareness is a very common thing."
>
> (CW 2, para. 113)

How to organise the data for analysis

Calculations

The objective now is to complete two calculations; conversion of decimals into 1/5 second and finding the median.

The Reaction times (already recorded digitally and entered in the RT column) are converted into 1/5 seconds and entered into the 1/5 column. Simply multiply the numbers in the RT column by rounding off the results to the nearest whole number and entering them into the 1/5 column. A calculator or the excel multiplication formula may be used.

The Excel process is as follows:

1 Enter the number to multiply by in some cell, say in C3 on the template.
2 Write a multiplication formula for the topmost cell in the column. That is =5*D3

3 Double-click the fill handle (lower right hand corner of the formula cell (D3) to copy the formula down the B column.

No.	SW	1/5	RT	RW	Rep	PRT	CI Code	CIT	Obj	Ego/c
33	glass	22	4,4	bottom	s		b, l, MW	1		√

Next, the PRTs must be calculated before entering them in the PRT column. The PRT's are the RT values which lie above the median.

The median is used instead of an arithmetic average (termed 'mean'), 'because the latter would be increased excessively by the few greatly lengthened response times caused by rejections or failures of association (Keiser 1980). Jung adopted this position after initially experimenting with the arithmetic mean.

The simplest way of calculating the median in Excel is to select the column labeled 1/5, which gives the reaction times in fifths of a second. Find a space on the spreadsheet separate from the tablet and click on it. Then enter the formula for finding the median, which is:

=MEDIAN(put the range of cells in here).
For example, =MEDIAN(B3:B53)

Then press Enter, and the answer will be displayed. The median in the case example is 18.

The PRTs are then recorded on the template, with the letter 'T', which is later counted as one complex indicator. some practitioners prefer to award more CIs to extremely long PRTs. The issue is discussed further in the research chapter, Chapter 12, of this volume.

No.	SW	1/5	RT	RW	Rep	PRT	CI Code	CIT	Obj	Ego/c
33	glass	22	4,4	bottom	s	T	b, l, MW	1		√

Make a chart

Next, make a chart of the Reaction Times as shown below, using the chart function in Word, WPS or Excel.

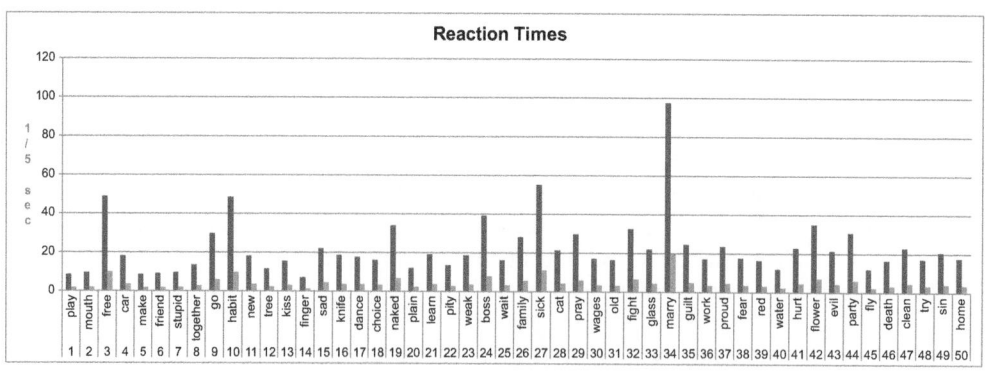

a List the PRTs.

The PRTs are then listed in a table, and each PRT is awarded 1 complex indicator in the CI column on the template.

34	marry	98
27	sick	55
3	free	49
10	habit	49
24	boss	39
42	flower	35
19	naked	34
32	fight	33
44	party	31
9	go	30
29	pray	30
26	family	28
35	guilt	25
37	proud	24
41	hurt	23
47	clean	23
15	sad	22
28	cat	22
33	glass	22
43	evil	22
49	sin	21
7	stupid	19
16	knife	19
21	learn	19
23	weak	19

Further data is gathered and organised in the three categories of stereotypes, association types and perseverations. These are the final preparatory steps before the next stage of preparation for the context interview, which is explained in the following chapter.

Stereotypes

Stereotypes are entered on the template as complex indicators. These are reaction words which occur three or more times as a response, counting the first and second run together. They are presented in a separate table. In this WAE, four stereotypes have been identified. They are: 'happy', 'brave' 'stupid' and 'experience'. They are recorded in the CI column.

Happy

No.	SW	1/5	RT	RW	Rep	PRT	CI Code	CIT	Obj	Sub
3	Free	49	9,8	happiness	Open sea*	T		3		√
7	Stupid	19	1,9	happy	fool			1		√
19	naked	34	6,8	happy	free	T	st	3		√

Brave

18	choice	16	3,2	problem	bravery		st	2	√
27	sick	55	11	brave	alone	T		4	√
32	fight	33	6,5	bravery	Titans	T		4	√
37	proud	24	4,7	brave	s	T	st	2	√
48	try	17	3,4	know	brave	T	MW, st	3	√

Stupid

7	stupid	19	1,9	happy	fool			1	√
22	pity	14	2,7	stupidity	s		st	1	√
23	weak	19	3,7	ignorant	not stupid	T	b, MW, st	5	√
38	fear	18	3,5	stupidity	flying			2	√
41	hurt	23	4,6	selfish	stupid	T	MW	5	√

Experience

11	new	18	3,6	challenge	experience		St, S,(p)	3	√
31	old	17	3,3	quality	experience		St, S	3	√
49	sin	21	4,1	experience	s		St, S	2	√

The next task is to add the complex indicators in the horizontal columns and to enter the total into the CI column. For example, Word 40, 'water', has four complex indicators. (Rep, b. MW and st).

No.	SW	1/5	RT	RW	Rep	PRT	CI Code	CI	Obj	Ego/c
40	water	12	2,4	depth	Open sea		b, MW, st	4		

We can now take a preliminary look at the SW, RW and Rep columns, noting that associations can be read across clusters (the columns and rows above). Each cluster may represent a complex, and it is interesting to note that the sets of words in each of three clusters have the connecting word 'happy' and that the 'Brave' and 'Experience' clusters are separated from each other and from the other two (with no connecting words). In the template can also be found words which have meaningful connections.

The completion of Stereotypes marks the conclusion of identifying CIs to be counted, and so at this point we can return to the WAE template and enter the total number for each SW into the CIT column (total number of complex indicators). Add (horizontally) the number of CIs for each SW and enter the results. Now the complete list of words can be organised and displayed in descending order (by the number of CIs) as follows:

No.	SW	RW	Rep	CIT
23	weak	ignorant	not stupid	6
48	try	know	brave	5
19	naked	happy	free	4
33	glass	bottom	s	4
41	hurt	selfish	stupid	4
3	free	happiness	Open sea	3
11	new	challenge	experience	3
13	kiss	slap	s	3
15	sad	unaware	alone	3
18	choice	problem	bravery	3
21	learn	freedom	richness	3
26	family	beehive	voice	3
27	sick	brave	alone	3
29	pray	desperate	weakness	3
31	old	quality	experience	3
32	fight	bravery	Titans	3
37	proud	brave	s	3
40	water	depth	open sea	3
43	evil	anger	man	3
7	stupid	happy	fool	2
9	go	far	s	2
10	habit	monotony	boredom	2
16	knife	pain	anatomy	2
22	pity	stupidity	s	2
25	wait	hope	losing time	2
28	cat	play	s	2
34	marry	cage	don't know	2
36	work	must	obligation	2
38	fear	stupidity	flying	2
49	sin	experience	s	2
5	make	chaos	shit	1
6	friend	V	s	1
8	together	sharing	s	1
20	plain	clever	cheek	1
24	boss	anarchy	s	1
30	wages	merit	s	1
35	guilt	mistake	s	1
42	flower	hippie sign	s	1
44	party	boredom	s	1
45	fly	fear	s	1
47	clean	FALSE	problem	1
50	home	tweed	s	1
1	Play	alley	s	
2	mouth	word	s	
4	car	end	s	
12	tree	stalk	s	
14	finger	direction	s	
17	dance	hall	s	
39	red	black	s	
46	death	inevitability	s	

It is possible but not necessary to display these graphically. From the above list, SW's with[2] more than two CIs have been selected in preparation for the Context Interview in part 2 of the experiment.

23	weak	6
48	Try	5
19	naked	4
33	glass	4
41	hurt	4
3	Free	3
11	New	3
13	Kiss	3
15	Sad	3
18	choice	3
21	learn	3
26	family	3
27	Sick	3
29	pray	3
31	Old	3
32	fight	3
37	proud	3
40	water	3
43	Evil	3

We can now return to the WAE template and classify the RWs into different association types.

Association types

Jung identified two types of association: Objective and Egocentric. These are recorded in the final two columns of the template but not counted as complex indicators.

No.	SW	1/5	RT	RW	Rep	PRT	CI Code	CIT	Obj	Ego/c
38	fear	18	3,5	stupidity	flying		S (p)	2		√
39	red	17	3,3	black	s		(p)		√	

1 Objective reactions are:

> Reactions of a subject whose attitude is essentially objective. At the same time the interpretation of the stimulus word as a question is in the background. There is a tendency to merely put words next to each other, partly in accordance with the law of similarity, partly according to current connections.
>
> (CW 2, para. 423)

Examples are: 'coffee/drink' and 'ink/pen'.

2 Egocentric reactions are 'those in which subjective memories prevail' (CW 2, para. 427). In this respect the attitude is egocentric. We have used the term 'subjective' in preference to 'egocentric', which now has negative connotations in popular usage.
When the Obj and Eco/c columns are completed, find the totals and note them.
3 If there is a preponderance of objective reactions, this might indicate that the client has an objective, well-adjusted stance in life. At the same time, it might indicate that emotional reactions are being

repressed. If there is a preponderance of subjective reactions, then a further classification is made into three sub-types: Simple constellation type, complex-constellation type and predicate type.

He further noted two constellation types; simple and complex:

Simple constellation type

This type is characterised by the emergence of numerous subjective experiences, mostly recent in origin and belonging for the most part to the field of everyday activities.

Examples are: 'coffee/Claridge's (place where the client usually drinks coffee) and 'ink/blazer' (the client's ball point pen recently leaked in their new jacket).

(These can be differentiated from meaningless responses when explanations are invited and given in the context interview.)

Complex-constellation type

Here, a complex is quite apparent. A common example is examination anxiety, where the client's responses reveal that[3] they feel that they are being interrogated and evaluated on a pass/fail basis. Jung discerns this type in the 'Reactions of a subject in whose reactions a feeling-toned complex appears quite openly' (CW 2, para. 429).

> A strong feeling-toned complex is characteristic of this mode of reaction. The stimulus-word is assimilated as a question; the experiment therefore bears the imprint of a conversation in which the subject has only a dim awareness of the current situation.
> (CW 2. para. 430)

Additionally he noted two (closely related) definition and predicate types:

Definition type

These may be discerned when definitions are frequently given as response words, for example 'play'/activity usually but not exclusively enjoyed by children. Jung observed that such responses sometimes indicated an 'intelligence complex' (CW 2, para. 985). The type might indicate an intellectual attitude.

Predicate type

The type can be recognised by the frequent use of evaluative and judging adjectives in reaction words. For example, 'coffee'/'lovely' and 'ink'/'messy'.

> Reactions of a subject who judges the object of the stimulus word from a personal point of view. The characteristic of this mode of reaction is an unusually strong personal participation, which leads to a constant evaluation of the object, usually with reference to themselves.
> (CW 2, para. 432–433)

The type might indicate an emotional attitude.

Perseverations

Perseverations of feeling-tone occur when a stimulus word has triggered a reaction word with a strong feeling tone (complex) which affects subsequent reaction words. It is typically observable on the chart of reaction times, where a PRT is followed by similar PRTs which decrease in a downward staircase as the client recovers from the disturbance. It is usually accompanied by complex indicators, often including tone of voice. Perseverations are not recorded as complex indicators. They are noted on the template by marking the first affected word with a capital P and subsequently affected words with a small p.

In this case the critical reaction may be quite unobtrusive, but the subsequent one has an abnormal character, in which the preceding reaction takes over the role of constellation (CW 2, para. 419).

No	SW	1/5	RT	RW	Rep	PRT	CI Code	CIT	Obj	Ego/c
34	marry	98	19,5	cage	don't know	T	(P)	2		√
35	guilt	25	4,9	mistake	s	T	(p)	1		√

Preliminary reflections

Once the complex indicators have been identified, counted and entered on the template, it is useful to note:

- If the 100-word list is used, note and explain any difference in the median reaction times of the first and second 50 words.
- The most common type of complex indicators
- How the client recovers after a complex indicator, referring to the perseverations (e.g. if the next word or words are disturbed)

Conclusion

The first part of the WAE is now concluded. We have covered the practical aspects of how to conduct the experiment, answering many frequently asked questions along the way. In the following Chapter 6, we consider the context interview.

Notes

1 Meier (1968) defined PRTs as two-fifths of a second or more above the median. We have found this method to be useful in providing a manageable (shorter) list of words for selection at the context interview. We recognise the relative importance of the complex indicator. It is also possible to make a separate standard distribution graph of the PRTs above the median.
2 This prioritises the list, shortening it to a manageable size before final selection.
3 Jung's quotes, personal and possessive, have been edited to non-gender-specific forms. This reflects our clinical experience of universal non-gender-specific application of the categories.

References

Jung, CG 1910, *Experimental Researches*, CW 2.
Kast, V 1980, *Das Assoziationsexperiment in der Therapuetischen Praxis*, Bonz Verlag, Feellbach-Offingen.
Keiser, RE 1980, 'Jung's Word Association Test: Response norms annd patterns of disturbances', *Master's Theses*. Paper 3252. <https://ecommons.luc.edu/luc_theses/3252>.

Additional Resources

Jung, CG 1909, 'Lectures delivered at the celebration of the twentieth anniversary of the opening of Clark University, September, 1909', *American Journal of Psychology*, vol. 31, pp. 219–269.
Jung, CG 1935, *The Tavistock Lectures*, CW 18.
Meier, C.A. 1968, *Die Empirie des Unbewusstens mit besonderer Berucksichtigung des Assoziationsexperiment von C. G. Jung*, Rascher, Zurich.

6 The context interview

John O'Brien

Preparing for the context interview

In the previous chapter a list of stimulus words attracting three or more complex indicators was given. While Jung suggested that all stimulus words with complex indicators could be explored, the first level of prioritisation is the words with three or more complex indicators. In practice we have found that prioritising the list to around 12 words is both sufficient and manageable. In any case, significant words with fewer indicators usually appear again in the responses given in the context interview.

Jung argued that the stimulus words should be re-presented in ascending order, i.e. with the least disturbing words first. This is to minimise the (perseveration) effect of highly disturbing stimulus words on responses to subsequent words during the context interview. While there are circumstances in which experimenters have reversed the word order in order to elicit a disturbance early on in the context interview, we concur with Jung on the grounds of (1) respect for the patient's defence mechanisms (caution against re-traumatisation) and (2) confidence in the psyche's natural tendency to respond favourably to a gentle and positive learning environment.

The aim of the experimenter is to facilitate this semi-structured process while keeping in mind that one of the objectives is to identify the complexes. Awareness of counter-transference both provide useful information and helps to avoid unwittingly leading the client in directions more related to the experimenter's complexes.

It is usual to begin the context interview with an introduction.

Guidance notes on the context interview

Example introduction

As with our other meetings, the context interview is confidential and subject to the code of ethics of my professional body and my institution (organisation, training institution or private practice).

As part of my own training experience, I am required to consult my training analyst/tutor for supervision and to present the experiment in a small professional group, where the same confidentiality rules apply. Your identity will not be revealed, and case material will be presented with sufficient changes to ensure that your identity remains protected.

After the meeting I would like to send you a transcript of the interview, and so I ask your permission to record it. It will be lightly edited to make it easy to read. This will help you to reflect privately on your reactions and associations and to make any further connections which you find meaningful and helpful before we (or I) build a map of the complexes we have discussed.

DOI: 10.4324/9781032716572-6

During this meeting we can go through the words which seemed to have been emotionally significant for you. These are the words which stimulated measurable emotional reactions significantly more or less than your own average (median). You might recall that I measured your reaction time to each stimulus word, the response words you gave and other verbal and non-verbal indicators of emotion.

I will tell you the stimulus word and ask you to explain the association(s) you made in a sentence or two. We will cover a dozen or so words during the next hour.

Given that the aim of the experiment is to promote self-discovery through the dialogue between the conscious and unconscious of the client and by noticing the constellated bi-personal themes, we have found the transcript to be a very useful tool for reflection of the client's content and for deepening the therapeutic alliance. At the feedback discussion we are frequently met with comments such as: Did I really say that? . . . I hadn't realised that I could remember such things . . . I had completely forgotten that.

It thus creates an additional (intermediate) reflection and cycle of learning in preparation for the feedback discussion.

Using video/audio recordings

In between sessions, the experimenter can study the video recording and note the response times and complex indicators with great precision. Furthermore, depending on the video quality, it is possible to observe and note changes in facial skin colour, pupil dilation and facial expressions accompanying verbal responses to stimulus words. For example, responses to picture stimuli have shown that dilation can indicate both pleasant and unpleasant emotional responses as observed and measured by galvanic skin responses (Bradley et al. 2008).

Interestingly, the client's perception and/or identification of the emotion accompanying changes in expression during the first interview may not always be accurate (Folz et al. 2022). This usually shows up most clearly in the context interview, which offers an opportunity for reflection, and it can be usefully revisited in the feedback session. Where expressions seem incongruent with the reported associated feelings, summary and reflection of expression and observed feeling can help. Also, naming feelings can usefully inform these discussions.

Interviewing method

While it is acceptable for the interview to be conducted with minimal prompting, we encourage the experimenter to use discretion and judgement to briefly summarise and reflect the content and feeling tone of the client's responses to provide a suitably comfortable environment to facilitate fuller expression and enhanced understanding. In the same vein, it is permissible to reflect one or two connections where this is suggested by the material presented by the client. The purpose of this is to stimulate the expansion of the client's own network of meaningful connections. In this way you are beginning to build elements for the complex map together while delivering therapeutic benefit.

In the following example, the context interview was recorded with hand-written notes. There is an extra section entitled 'examination' which has been filled in by the experimenter after the context interview was completed. These are her own notes which she used as aides memoire for her presentation. (If this method is chosen, the legal obligations of freedom of information should be kept in mind, alongside the paramount concern for the client's well-being).

Example of context interview

Stimulus word: Free

Free space. No barriers, constraints, simply peace within, peaceful, blue, infinite, big, not without rules, but without norms. Simply that it is peace and endlessly big and that you draw happiness and energy from it. A house on the island. H. comes to mind where we used to go all the time. When I look – I see a lighthouse to the right and a huge space behind. I always wondered what was there . . . I feel peace when I see that broadness. We used to go there between 7 and 22 years of age both summer and winter. I don't think I am very free. First I do not have a freedom to do all the time what I want. Before I usually did what I thought I had or should do. It is better now but I was rarely me. Freedom is when you are who you are and somebody either loves you or not. To be who you are is freedom for me.

Examination

Her inner position and state-of-being, where one can be open to experience life and develop is also elemental – 'open sea' which could indicate the connection to the unconscious and access to it. It is important to mark that the way these references are given does not indicate unruly chaotic expanding energy, but rather the one that provides peace within natural rules. I am inclined to understand this level as ego–self relation.

The ancestral-developmental (trans-generational) level view also provides a bridge between collective and individual meaning. D's experiences between 7–22 years of age are potentially serving as a 'lighthouse' function of her psyche; they seem to carry also positive experiences of her childhood drawing the allying forces supporting D's ability for insight. The light house is an important point of topographical relevance for D's psyche: It is not the private house on the island, it is on the ground (not the water), it sheds the light on darkness helping ships sailing on the water to orient and be safe. It seems that when in the 'lighthouse position', D can see what is going on, safe from the potentially overwhelming contents in the private house, but connected to it, having a firm ground underneath from the place she observes/experiences life, and at the same time very closely connected to the unconscious supporting the navigation of the content that comes from there by the light of insight. It would be interesting to explore what are the qualities of experiences and inheritance that D got there in her biological life and how her parental and ancestral images live in her supporting her journey.

Reflecting upon D's last comments:

'*I don't think I am very free. First I do not have a freedom to do all the time what I want. Before I usually did what I thought I had or should do. It is better now but I was rarely me. Freedom is when you are who you are and somebody either loves you or not. To be who you are is freedom for me*'.

I wonder, given her dreams and reactions, whether she can be free only when she herself becomes aware of who she is – for this period of her wounded self and accepting it?

Stimulus word: Kiss

I constantly have that sound 'sljap'. I hated when my aunts and alike 'lick' me and hug me . . . oh how cute she is, oh how sweet and then they would pinch my cheek . . . uh it annoyed me enormously! I got fewest kisses from my father, everybody else was 'licking' me and I hated it. As a child I did not like to speak and they made me speak all the time. There was a teacher in my school who constantly forced me to speak (I was 4 years old). Even today I am quiet in a company of people I do not know well. I remember that she was pulling my hair so much, I still wouldn't speak, at the end when she stopped I told her 'You ass!' and then she started hugging me and kissing me so that I felt sick. Once I got beaten by my father when I was 8–9 years old with his belt and an hour after he came to me crying and apologising, he thought I ran away from home and there was a mad client who was threatening him . . . he got afraid that something happened to me. When he approached to me to kiss me I hated it and I still hear that 'sljap' sound . . . (she was quiet for a while, as if thinking of something else). It has nothing to do with romantic male–female kisses; I like those kinds of kisses.

Examination

Responses to the word 'kiss' seem to bring negative feelings mainly related to dishonesty, pretence and being hurt (aggression) behind that pretence. In all the examples D gave regarding to kisses are people that overtly or covertly hurt her, emotionally and physically. One does hear longing in D's offhand comment I got fewest kisses from my father, everybody else was licking me – as if she was expecting from her father (role?) not to execute such behavior. What these responses bring to mind is passive and open aggression, of which she was a victim during her entire childhood and also later in her life in a repetitive pattern. At the same time it seems that kiss is a token of true connection for D. We find again the element of water.

Stimulus word: **Naked**

No constraints, it associates me of that freedom, nothing is constraining me. I never wanted to be naked; I remember being 3 years old and people looking at me . . . I remember my mother entering the kitchen in her night gown and my father shouting at her to 'cover herself' and that she should be ashamed to show herself like that in front of me (7–8 years of age). On my birthday my mother took me to the photographer to take a picture of me. She dressed me in the clothes I disliked and when I was 14 years of age I said I did not want to do it anymore. It was like doing a sentence, I cried every time. It was important to my mother that I looked as a doll. The only thing I liked was my knitted socks. They always went to people (and took me with them) without children. She liked combing my hair and making different coiffures. I was frustrated I couldn't be me. My only freedom was when I was with an animal and did whatever I wanted with it. My mother never bought anything new for me, I did not have my own coat till I was 16, I was inheriting other people's clothes. Nowadays I buy clothes uncontrollably and never have any. First thing she bought for me was a tweed jacket when I was 15. It was important to my father that I was dressed like a proper girl. My parents were never naked in front of me. I remember my potty. I had problems defecating (3–4 years of age). They made me sit on the potty for hours. Till 3 years ago, I was not able to empty my bowels regularly.

Examination

The theme of being herself continues here as well, shedding an additional light to Anima–Persona relationship. In respect to the relationship with her mother, there is a pattern of trying to please the external demands to be accepted on one side, and at the same time not mirroring her genuine personality. In addition to her feeling inadequate, in D's thinking there is something wrong with her one can think of negative Animus who is misleading in nature. Inhibitions of expressing herself seem to be incorporated through the physiological dimension as well, with an important change 3 years ago. One pivotal connection to the true nature that D never seized to have was with animals. They are closest beings to her in life even now and her closest family, perhaps signaling still, on the symbolic level, her deepest need for resonating with nature. D's dogs have been winners of many trophies, always among first in dogs' exhibitions . . . One might think of 'dolls' and 'finger-direction' reaction . . . (SW 14).

Stimulus word: Boss

I hate rules (norms), especially if I do not understand them. I did not like them as a child; I do not like them now. I hate when somebody tells me you have to. It took me many years to understand that I don't have to; it is I want or do not want to, not I have to. I always had rules imposed on me (you must not sit at the table with grown up, you have to go to the shops, you have to be quiet, you must not talk back . . ., while you are under my roof it has to be like I want . . .). Where there are too many rules imposed – anarchy is created. In my work I always tried to develop and go up the ladder very quickly, to be one step above from others, so that those imposed rules are lesser, so that I could be more creative, make a decision not only obey.

Examination

The toll of too strict Animus, apparently in both of her parents (and aunts and uncles from both sides) and negative feminine in setting the boundaries that constipated her expression and natural flow of life energy could be seen in D's challenges with superiors. The reaction she will get towards them is 'anarchy'. She would find herself in a position of a rebellion against the rules, she would feel the rules limiting and suffocating expression and often highly unjust. It is also interesting that D would have people 'above' her who would be very different to her and probably of the opposite type. There is a curious development of the 'qualities' in her 'bosses' through her career – from really abusive ones to a person she works for at the moment (seems to be dominant thinking type) whom she disagrees but respects highly and is able to disagree with high presence of emotional charge but at the same time with the objective perspective and empathy.

Stimulus word: Family

It was always like in a beehive. Always too many people, my mother was 'tied' to her sister and I am absolutely positive that she loved them more than me. Aunt and uncle were teachers, extremely stern and my mother always went to them to solve their problems (for example their children ran away from home). It was always them (my cousins) who were better, harder working, created more in their lives (in fact – they are now miserable, they actually have nothing) I always had to be like them. I always hated them, even nowadays I do not have any contact with them. On the other side – my father had a brother with two children, nobles, good pupils, sportsmen . . . I had to be like them as well. I do not have a contact with them either. VOICE – noise: Gossiping, and then my mother and father would quarrel – from my father side very 'fine' and well educated, opposite from my mother side . . . always many voices, that were not ours. If it wasn't for my mother's huge bond with her sister . . . maybe my mother and father would stay longer together. My mother and father never had a common bedroom. I was once making spots with a stick on a freshly painted wall, my mother bit me so badly. She has never apologised to me. And so many times she was not right.

Examination

Here we got some stronger light on to the familial unconscious setup, forces traveling transgenerationally, charged with such a high potential – embodied in D's mother suicide. D said that her mother could not stand the pain any longer and decided to stop it. Her mother stopped. (It is perhaps worthwhile noticing that it was D's left breast that was diagnosed with cancer). It is interesting that D is working with 40–200 children who are creating music through improvisation and she always comments with a smile that it is very noisy and 'busy'. D speaks about a beehive, many different voices, noise and high frequency, high fluctuation of different energies. In her childhood it resulted with dissonant energy (parents would quarrel); in her present life the children make a high quality musical out of lot of 'noise'. I also think of a symbol of beehive for quite a few ancient civilizations when they reached their peak of prosperity and harmony, as a potential of development. I am also thinking about the dissonance between two different qualities that should be in a harmonious marriage: Village, 'ordinary', more simple people (D's mother family) and educated, 'sophisticated', urban (father's family) and how this disharmony was internalised in D's psyche. Reflecting upon D's words given here, perhaps it is that the developing of the raw material was interrupted so it remained in storming phase creating a neurotic circle. On the other side none of the families supported D's love for animals so through D's strongest devotion to animal care the gradient for this familial oppressed energy came into being.

D's last comment, apparently disconnected to the previous context, provoke an image of deliberate 'spoiling' the perfection in Islamic architecture – nothing in nature is one-sided. Furthermore, as if D wanted to add some content to the fresh beginning, continuing the process of the renovation of her parents' intimacy . . .

Stimulus word: Sick

I thought of not telling you but I will tell you. I got diagnosed with the breast cancer. I was in Belgrade at that time. When I went to oncology institute I wanted to die when I saw the cancer patients there. For quite a long while I did not want to do anything regarding the illness, just to let it go in its own course. Then I decided to go to Sweden. I stayed at my friend and his wife after the surgery and was on chemo therapy. It was tough but I made it. I was alone and nobody except my two best friends knew. I did not mind dying, just the pain. I had to be brave. Everything will pass . . . I have to go on. If I stop I will get ill. The only thing that matters is that nobody looks at me.

Examination

D's comments remind me of the beach scene and nakedness – when she did not want to be naked, feeling shy (shame?) because something was wrong with her . . . Now she actually misses a part of her body and people can actually see it. Apart from her very closest friends, nobody knows that she was ill at all. The key themes here could be pain, loneliness – absence of support, need to move, and hope for the good outcome. I am thinking of the negative mother complex but also of a positive father complex (in the sense that things will turn out well). D's father seemed to be harsh, violent, highly critical but also he was the one who 'could' in the family. He was enterprising and was able to execute things perhaps in opposition to her mother who eventually stopped. I am also thinking about D's connection to animals – the connection to the innate knowledge of nature per excellence (healing power for ex.), therefore there could be a presence of a positive mother complex as well.

Stimulus word: Pray

To pray for what. For health. Every time I was supposed to pray and light the candles I did, but . . . I am the one who can decide whether I will be ok or not. I do not understand people who find a church when they are not well. If I do not have peace with myself no church will help me. I do believe (not in priests), I am not a non-believer. I do not brag that I am a believer it is disgusting to me – bljak (like sljap). I do not believe that any of them is a true believer, it is all – mimicry.

BRAVE? – Me . . .

Examination

I read here an awareness and maturity of a person who learned from life experience that there is a lot to be done with one's 'destiny' if one is aware and works on one's own world discovering powers that are there. It feels it is with pinch of sorrow (bitterness?) because D had to learn it due to absence of support – she was left to her own devices early in her life. In this respect I am also thinking of a sense of anger and longing in her reaction towards people who do find sense and help in going to church when they are not well – as if she is bothered by their ability to find comfort in the forces outside. Developmentally, it is the silence and dissonance as a result of the attempts of early childhood tuning. Negative mother and critical (abusive) father. But she is a believer. Again, there is a deeper force behind the negative experiences giving her support and hope.

Stimulus word: Marry

Nothing comes, but absolutely nothing. Point blank. I do not have a person, nor situation related to this. I do have a problem, guaranteed. Why when you marry, why do people always have incredible urge that now something needs to change. We are married now, now something needs to change. I fall in love with somebody with all the faults . . . I wanted to change, but not somebody else changing me. I did change by my own will for somebody before . . . what came to me then! I would consciously stop myself wanting to change somebody, to adjust. My friend has a habit to chew a toot-pick. My female friend, his partner keeps telling him – take the toot-pick out, stop eating that much . . . grumping, grumping or being angry and silent . . . that is marriage. A cage – because of this grumping. Returning the images of my mother and father and also some of my relationships. Why do I care . . . why one has to get married in order to be socially successful?! Are you married? – they ask me, and if I am not, it must be something wrong with me . . .

Examination

D herself makes a connection between her feeling towards marriage and her experiences of her parents' marriage. Here is again the theme of being herself and not somebody else in relation to the expectation of the other. D is also aware of her own need to change others and the positive willingness to change/adjust herself in a relationship when it is her conscious decision. The resistance to be who she is not because of the expectation of others is striking perhaps reflecting the huge suffering and pain she went through. The defense against that pain embodied in a token of a relationship as such – the marriage is obvious. It is also obvious D's wish to be in a relationship where she would be accepted for who she is. I wonder whether the amount of pain and the need to protect herself against it inhibited her to fight for the relationship she enjoyed so much? Or/and was it her (unconscious) feeling of something actually wrong with her that made her give up on something that fulfilled her so much? She cannot be good enough for him, nor for the happiness she experiences, it cannot last, so it is better to end it now . . .? Since she had to be brave and not stop (meet her pain, have pity), could it be that 'what is wrong with her' now is the wounded D appearing on the stage? Can she 'marry' her, love her and support her for what she is?

Stimulus word: Party

I simply cannot recall a party or wedding that I had a good time. Weddings – kitsch parades. Parties – it comes down to talking to people I came with, drinking beer and smoking dope. And if among those 50 people there is somebody 'smart' and starts talking . . ., I immediately get quiet. I like to go out, I like to get together over dinner and talk with my friends, but not with 50 people . . . I do love my birthday, I make it the way I like, gather people I like . . . At the parties everybody speaks at the same time, I can't properly hear anybody . . . I did not like the disco clubs either. Smaller circle of friends I like.

I feel safe, people who will not mind if I spill something on me, drink a bit more . . . I love demonstrations. Anarchy. I love concerts. I would marry The Englishman tomorrow, because he was genuine. With him I have never felt him wanting to change me, or laugh at me if I say something silly. We could speak about everything. We laughed a lot, I always loved to go out with him. He did not like 50 people parties either. I did not have to make myself beautiful in order for him to like me. Happiness. Then I would define marriage as freedom and big space. If only I could have that feeling again – to be able to be quiet in peace, to be myself . . .

Examination

Here I find the circle of meaning rounding off with the return, or re-ligare to the collective level: Open sea, peace, happy. To be herself. She is describing party of non-listening/hearing each other, noise, which reminds me of the beehive, voices and responses to 'family'. The way D reflects on this SW, especially in the semantic sequence, potentially reflects a formula of having positive experience of life: Having different voices expressed, listened to and heard properly brings marriage and a potential party – joie de vivre.

Stimulus word: Hurt

That somebody who is going to hurt you must be stupid. I do not understand how they have time to do these things – to hurt somebody. My father and my mother . . . such insults and bad words . . . What do I gain if I tell you – 'you are so ugly' . . . And then they would put me in the middle and ask me who was right. I will tell you directly what I think or I will keep quiet. I think it is a total stupidity either if I allow somebody to hurt me – somebody who will say to me something like how could you allow yourself to be so fat . . . My father used to tell me all the time how stupid I was. My partner in Sweden used to tell me that I was stupid and brought me to the point when I actually thought either that I was ignorant or really stupid. It was only when I met The Englishman . . . My partner apologised later, I understood that he was not feeling ok in general that it was not me. It is selfish that I feel better if I hurt you. It is not clear to me and I do not want it to be clear to me. And who am I to judge . . . I do not like when people insult somebody. I feel sadness and if it is really a bad insult I get angry and then I want justice to be done.

Examination

D's words above seem very rational, ethical and proper. 'Too' rational. I am thinking that maybe this could be a defense against actually expressing her anger and a potential depressive structure. I do not like when people insult somebody. I feel sadness and if it is really a bad insult I get angry and then I want justice to be done. D's reaction to aggression towards her is sadness (result of her expression of anger was severely censored when she was a child). It has to be really a bad 'hurt' in order that she demands justice. I am thinking of D setting boundaries in her life and also about her illnesses. D is spending majority of her time caring about children that are hurt, trying to get justice for them. The reaction 'stupid' sheds additional light how powerful (and somehow 'final', non-discussible) that word is in her experience, terminating any attempt for anger to come out. I wonder that at some point the power of it helped not to stop . . . Perhaps it is the time now for her to carefully open to compassion for her own suffering and not feel stupid.

Stimulus word: Flower

Oh yes! Flowers associated me with the smile and then to the hippy sign. Everything related to flowers calms me down, I love to work with flowers. I love to have flowers, it is beautiful and gentle. Poppy seed flower, ever so gentle creature, the petals, you need to take care of them and then it rewards you with something so beautiful. I could not pick a poppy-seed flower, ever. There is a fairy tale related with a poppy seed, ever so tender, petals, rewarding you with something so beautiful. I could never pick a poppy seed flower. There is a fairytale . . . It closes in the morning and opens in the evening, there are 3 petals, does not last long, few days, flower of May, sometimes September . . . Maiden's veil. Don't laugh, lasts long, burnt by the sun, I took it back in to the shade. I grow flowers, the one called 'contempt' in my language is my favorite plant. I never know what kind of flower will come up, plus you don't need to water it. It is so tender, you think it will die, but it is actually so endurable . . . flowers from lilac to white, entire spectrum.

Examination

Who is D? How she grows and flourishes? As if this was 'a big dream' that we usually do not analyse, rather just allowing scents of psyche to enrich our life in entire spectrum . . . D could not remember which one. I am thinking about Vasilisa The Wise and the poppy seed as a food of dead – lowering down the control of consciousness, ability to be and relax . . .?

Relevant research

The context interview in the WAE training protocol is essential to the experiment/test.

Firstly, it enables a structured conversation between the experimenter and client, during which the experimenter can deploy summary and reflection of content and tone and authentically communicate with empathy, respect and genuineness, these relationship skills ranking very highly for psychotherapeutic effectiveness in the Swiss Charta publication.

Secondly, it enables the client/patient to contextualise response words in a sentence or two. This is especially important where responses are regarded by the experimenter as idiosyncratic or bizarre and classified as meaningless. While it is acknowledged that the preponderance of idiosyncratic responses might indicate thought disorders, such words might appear meaningful when the client has the opportunity to put them into a sentence and explain the association. This is highly relevant where word association tests are used as adjuncts in the diagnosis of schizophrenia. The patient's ability to explain the association or otherwise can aid differential diagnosis of positive and negative schizophrenia (Johnson 1990) in the following way. With positive schizophrenia the patient is frequently able to find and convey meaning given the opportunity to contextualise the response word and to explain the association, whereas with negative schizophrenia this is not the case.

To the extent that meaningless responses become meaningful to the experimenter, the patient's associative world is validated by the recognition of the experimenter, and through 'shared meaning', both the therapeutic alliance is strengthened and psycho-social invalidation and marginalisation are reduced. In these respects the context interview provides therapeutic benefit. (This chimes with our client feedback and feedback from clients of candidates in training.)

It also enables clients/patients to become aware of their own association networks and, in the case of post ego-formation complexes, to bring them to consciousness, thus making them accessible for reflection. We can say that in this way there is a differentiation between the ego complex and the fundamental (for example parental) complexes. In the case of pre-ego formation insult and injury it is more difficult to raise the networks to consciousness as they are generally pre-verbal and feeling based, taking the form of representations of interactive generalisations (see RIGs in Chapter 9). In these cases, resonance, silent witnessing and reflection on feeling and image work are often helpful.

References

Bradley, M, Miccoli, L, Escrig, M, Lang, P 2008, 'The pupil as a measure of emotional arousal and autonomic activation', *Psychophysiology*, vol. 45, no. 4, pp. 602–607.

Folz, J, Fiacchino D, Nikolić, M 2022, 'Reading your emotions in my physiology? Reliable emotion interpretations in absence of a robust physiological resonance', *Affective Science*, vol. 3, pp. 480–497.

Johnson, E 1990, 'Word Association and Schizophrenia symptomatology', *Dissertations & Theses*, William & Mary. Paper 1539625640. Visited February 12, 2024. <doi: 10.21220/s2-b2fm-1v43>.

Additional Resources

Karsten, W 2015, 'Measuring facial expression of emotion', *Dialogues in Clinical Neuroscience*, vol. 17, no. 4, pp. 457–462.

Lepori, D 2015, 'Introduction to WAE', [Seminar notes], C G Jung Institute, Zurich.

Stern, D 1985, *The Interpersonal World of the Infant: A View from Psychoanalysis and Developmental Psychology*, Basic Books, New York.

Tschuschke, V, Koemeda-Lutz, M, Schlegel, M 2014, *PAP-S-Rating-Manual (PAP-S-RM): Rating Manual for the Objective Evaluation of Therapeutic Interventions of Psychotherapists Based on Various Theoretical Concepts*, Schriftenreihe der Schweizer Charta für Psychotherapie, Zurich.

7 Map of complexes

Nada O'Brien

Map of complexes

The most important thing to bear in mind throughout the AE is that the words with complex indicators are the *matter of the living soul*. We are not dealing with simple, intellectual concepts or mere notions of reason; each 'word' is an image, impregnated with vital energy, an image with great significance for the individuation process; each word is what Jung calls a *living symbol*. Ultimately, the very source of the vital charge of the images which manifest as words with complex indicators are archetypes. Therefore, as with any other narrative which is a manifestation of the unconscious, the approach to the very engagement and interpretation is fourfold: Sensing, thinking, feeling and intuitive perspectives must be considered.

The process of articulating the map of complexes is a process of articulating a map of activated forces of psyche which are manifested to consciousness as 'words'. These 'words' are symbols, thus they are surfacing multilayered psychic content – from the individual, familial, cultural and collective unconscious. Therefore, the approach to articulating the map of complexes is similar to the approach to dream interpretation. The dream scenes, characters, plots, etc. are interrelated in a profoundly meaningful way, so is the map of complexes showing not only the interrelatedness of the specific words within one complex but also the connection between different complexes as well as the *overall movement of psychic energy constellated in the current individuation phase*. This overall movement of psychic energy informs us about the teleological function of psyche.

Process of articulating the map

The facts

We gather all the words with complex indicators. We consider adding the key words which emerged in the Context interview to the initial words. In order to differentiate their origin, we suggest writing them in a different colour or style.

Example

Free Ticket Work

Father Car *Engine* o *Heart* Speed *Family*

Hybrid Mobility

Adaptation Survival

Breaking rules Creative

Evil Money Wages *Limitations*

Expectations bigger & bigger

Fear *Running away*

Internal relation of the words: Value and logic

We look at the words with the highest libidinal charge – such as the words with the highest number of complex indicators. We look at the *value order* in the sense which word/s (image/s) are *central* for the constellated theme and which words are orbiting around these central issue/s, which words seem more or most 'important' (accentuated or bear most 'weight') and which words are in a way adding to or accompanying this central value. We try to discern a hierarchy of importance based on value.

We then look for the *logical order* of the words in terms of the ways they are related to each other; we are articulating the structure of the complex visually presenting several planes: Semantic logic of relatedness, their proportional relation, internal dynamics of the words (how are they 'moving').

Example

Free Ticket **Work**

Father Car *Engine* Go **Heart** Speed *Family*

Hybrid Mobility

Adaptation **Survival**

Breaking rules Creative

Evil Money Wages ***Limitations***

Expectations bigger & bigger

Fear ***Running away***

Meaning: Constellated themes

We now look at this structure and ponder the meaning of the complex and its unconscious background; What is the underlying '*theme*' of the cluster of words which connects them all together? Based on the theme we discern we give the cluster a name:

Example

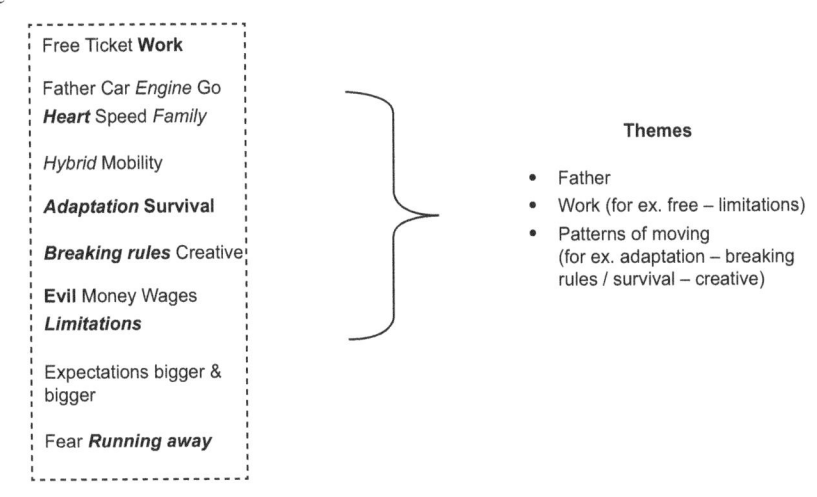

```
Free Ticket Work
Father Car Engine Go
Heart Speed Family
Hybrid Mobility
Adaptation Survival
Breaking rules Creative
Evil Money Wages
Limitations
Expectations bigger & bigger
Fear Running away
```

Themes
- Father
- Work (for ex. free – limitations)
- Patterns of moving
  (for ex. adaptation – breaking rules / survival – creative)

We then take a next step in discerning the meaning by taking into consideration the constellated theme in the context of different complex types. The framework of complex types is presented in the next subchapter as 'Complex landscapes' (Lepori 2015) in order to illustrate the process of discerning the deeper meaning of constellated complexes and further articulation of the map; It is important to emphasise that the 'landscape' presents only certain chosen types of complexes for the purpose of illustration, while in the process of actual work it does not need to be limited to the examples that follow.

Complex landscapes

Lepori (2015) outlines the 'main complexes' (Ego, Mother, Father, Siblings), as well as the 'emotional centres of significance'. She further specifies these different types of complexes, differentiating the 'positive' and 'negative' aspects. (It is important to note that, like the other unconscious content, the complexes are not in themselves negative but need integrating; see CW 6, para. 925 onwards.) These specifications given in complex landscapes are only examples of orientation points in the process of discerning further the types of complexes. In order to develop proper understanding and sensitisation to different complexes, it is necessary to study Jung's work on these topics as well as postjungian research on complexes.

Mother complex

- Positive
  - Emotional security
  - Protection
  - Recognition
- Negative
  - Solitude, separation
  - Helplessness, being at the mercy
  - Basic emotion of not getting enough to live

Father complex

- Positive
  - Good self-esteem
  - Confidence in one's own competence
  - Comfort in shaping one's own life

- Negative
  - Feeling of inferiority
  - Feeling of annihilation
  - Merciless self-criticism

Sibling complex (Lee et al. 2019)

Sibling solidarity and Shadow Carriers
Birth order, sex, temperament and the quality of parental presence play a part in constellating the intense polarities of sibling relationships:

- Competition and cooperation
- Admiration and envy
- Hierarchy and partnership
- Aggression and intimacy

The dynamics of early sibling relationships is carried on throughout life externally between self and other internally between ego and unconscious.

Ego complex

- Boundaries between *I* and *Other* (internal: regarding the inner psychic forces; external regarding the environment); questions regarding inflation/deflation and ego integrity; ego stability/coherence
- Ways of relating (internally – with the unconscious; externally – with the environment)
- Ways of adaptation; one-sidedness/rigidity – openness/flexibility
- Sense of identity and continuity
- Ways of 'reality-check' (including the 'evoked other'; stern . . .)

We now reflect on the complex we discerned a theme for (for example 'Poverty') and named accordingly in order to specify the type of the complex further.

Negative mother complex
Homelessness
Stinginess
'POVERTY'
Constant worries about money

Map of complexes   47

It is important to bear in mind that there might be several different clusters of words which will have different *themes* but belong to the same type of a complex from the deeper unconscious layer perspective. For example:

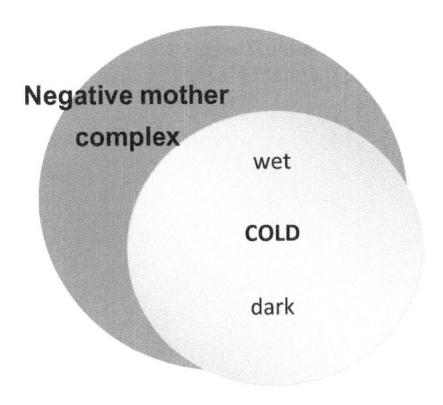

Negative mother complex

wet

COLD

dark

When the process is completed with all the complexes, we then take a look at the dynamic between them. How are they related? How are they affecting each other? We present the dynamics visually in the map.

Finally, we should consider the *movement* of the complexes: Is there a notion of development/regression with regards to certain individual complexes and or a group of complexes? Rigidity and stuckness (lack of motion)? Is there a sense of overall movement of the complexes in the landscape?

Example

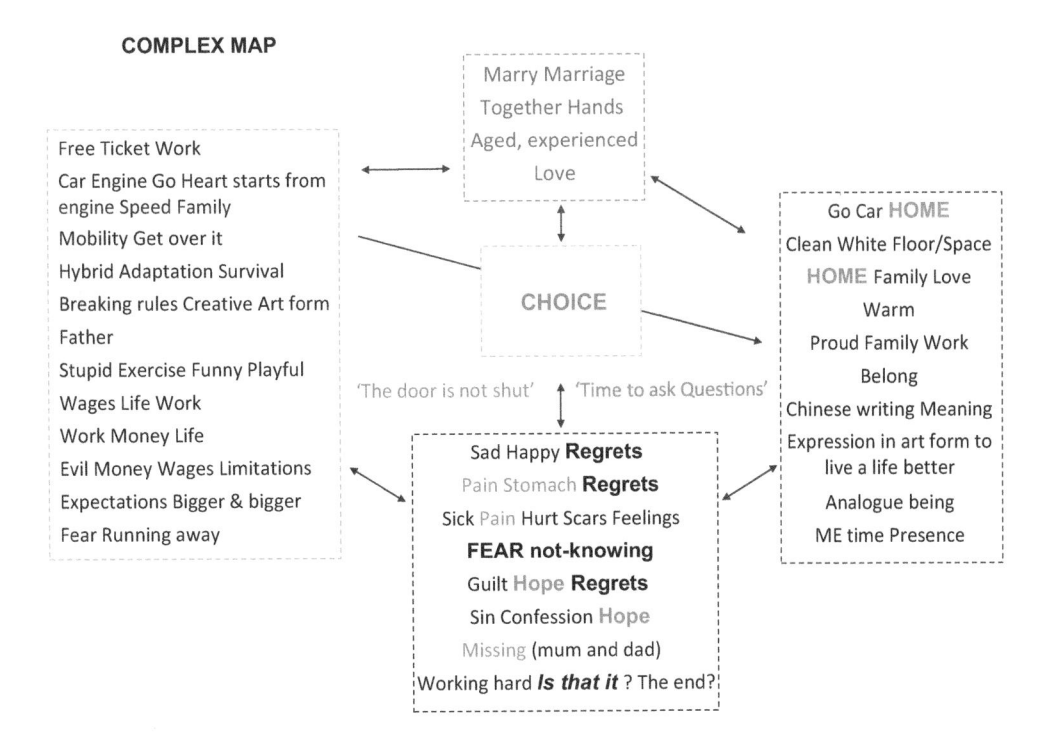

COMPLEX MAP

Free Ticket Work
Car Engine Go Heart starts from engine Speed Family
Mobility Get over it
Hybrid Adaptation Survival
Breaking rules Creative Art form
Father
Stupid Exercise Funny Playful
Wages Life Work
Work Money Life
Evil Money Wages Limitations
Expectations Bigger & bigger
Fear Running away

Marry Marriage Together Hands Aged, experienced Love

CHOICE

'The door is not shut'   'Time to ask Questions'

Sad Happy **Regrets**
Pain Stomach **Regrets**
Sick Pain Hurt Scars Feelings
FEAR not-knowing
Guilt Hope **Regrets**
Sin Confession Hope
Missing (mum and dad)
Working hard ***Is that it*** ? The end?

Go Car HOME
Clean White Floor/Space
HOME Family Love
Warm
Proud Family Work
Belong
Chinese writing Meaning
Expression in art form to live a life better
Analogue being
ME time Presence

References

Jung, CG 1921/1990, *Psychological Types*, CW 6.
Jung, CG 2000, *The Collected Works of C. G. Jung* (CW), eds. H Read, M Fordham, G Adler and W McGuire, trans. RFC Hull, Princeton University Press, Princeton.
Lee, J, Marchiano, L, Stewart, D 2019, 'Sibling complexes', *This Jungian Life*, [podcast], <https://podcasts.apple.com/ca/podcast/episode-089-sibling-complexes/id1376929139?i=1000459369655>.
Lepori, D 2015, 'Introduction to WAE', [Seminar notes], C G Jung Institute, Zurich.

8 Building an interpretation hypothesis and therapeutic use of WAE

Nada O'Brien, John O'Brien

Building an interpretation hypothesis

There are several ways to build an interpretation hypothesis. Some practitioners prefer to entitle this section 'synopsis' and give a summary account of their findings and reflections so far. Others prefer to use the more formal title of 'interpretation hypothesis', detailing the observed complexes, the psycho-dynamics in play and offering a tentative diagnosis based either on common factors (see Chapter 11) and/or DSM/ICD classifications. Alternatively, a Jungian psycho-social diagnostic assessment hypothesis might be preferred. The choice will depend on the professional training and orientation of the experimenter. The interpretation hypothesis can then be discussed with client or patient as appropriate. As it is a natural precursor to a further conversation about the possible adjustment of the aims of therapy and the agreed plan (even if this is open-ended), it is advisable, where possible, to discuss the interpretation with the patient, using as much of the patient's own language and terms as possible. This helps to prevent unnecessary distancing in the therapeutic alliance while staying close to the patient's actual experiences and representations thereof.

The hypothesis is built with reference to the following data points.

- The findings from parts 1 and 2 of the experiment
- The anamnesis
- The context interview
- Interim reflections of the patient
- Transference, counter/transference and *field* phenomena
- Re-constellated themes in training and supervision
- Typological preferences
- Map of complexes

In advanced post-qualification training, synchronicities and recursive analysis may also be used (see Note on further research in Appendix 1).

The interpretation process of the WAE results is multifold. Bearing in mind that all the words in the map are relevant images, we need approach to them in the same complex way we would approach images surfaced via dreams or other types of artifacts of the unconscious; we notice the effect the image on us, our own spontaneous reactions (including our body, emotions, fantasy); we ponder the deeper background of the images in terms of the amplification method; we consider the client's own reflections they provided in the context, and furthermore we consider the wider context of the client's situation and life history (including dreams and events which occurred in the period of the WAE). In this complex process we look at the ancestral and cultural layers of the unconscious background of the complexes, and ultimately we ponder the archetypal force central to each complex. We also consider the emotional centres of complexes, asking: What does the affect want? (Lepori 2015):

Fear

Challenge: Identity change
Defense/Resistance: Withdrawal, Counter phobia, Avoidance

Anger

Challenge: Setting boundaries, Differentiation
Defense/Resistance: Repression, Aggression, Control

Shame and Guilt   (Socialisation)
Challenge: Recognition and Responsibility
Defense/Resistance: Persevering in the identification with the child or parent role

Lepori (2015) further emphasises that flexibility in handling affects is an indicator for emancipation from the parental complexes. We can consider this as an empirical token of the client's progress.

We then enrich the map with this new information and then look at the map in order to discern the overall dynamics, the archetypal plot constellated for the client. We ask the question: Where does the energy go to? We ponder about the teleological perspective indicated in the map. These hypothetical conclusions are the most important information for future therapeutic work with the client.

Interpretation hypothesis outline

Although the examples of interpretation hypothesis will differ based on the multifold factors stated so far, the skeleton of the interpretation hypothesis must contain the following considerations:

- Description of the detected complexes
  - Outline the process from the constellated themes
  - Describe how the complexes manifest in the client's life (consider also Lepori's notion on affects)
  - Describe the client's management of the complexes: Level of awareness, defence/coping mechanisms
  - Include the developmental perspective (see Chapter 9)
- Archetypal dimension
  - Describe the archetypal source of complexes
  - Apply the amplification method, focusing on archetypal images
  - Consider the archetypal dynamics – for example constellated fairy-tale/myth 'plots'
  - Note your reaction to these images and reflect on your role and relationship with the client (transference, counter-transference, *field*)
- Teleological perspective
  - Describe the overall movement of the libidinal energy
  - Reflect on the teleological perspective as indicated by the WAE findings

- Therapeutic indications
  - Reflect how the findings of the WAE inform about the further therapeutic work with the client; take a special consideration of the symbols which occurred in the process of the WAE and use them as a guide. This can be articulated as a separate chapter of your WAE document.

Therapeutic use of WAE

As noted, like in any work with the unconscious, the images will affect the analyst. For example, when a client shares a dream, it will immediately produce reactions and personal images for the analyst to be aware of before he explores further the client's own information and perspective on the dream. As we know from the theory and practice of analytical psychology, these personal reactions of the analyst are not always aligned with the meaning of the dream for the patient. Rather the analyst's own issues are provoked by the client's dream. The same is relevant for the interpretation process of the WAE. Therefore, ideally, the interpretation process should include the client's participation. Bearing in mind that the words surfaced by the WAE are the substance of the living soul, the most beneficial work framework would be to facilitate the client's personal engagement with them. By that, we do not imply a high level intellectual understanding of the results but a deeply soul human connection communicating with the client in symbolic language. Therefore, the optimal method would comprise the same type of communication, for example, involving fantasy:

- The client is given the clusters of words from the initial stage of articulating the map (without naming the complex).
- The client is then asked to look at each cluster as if it is alive and then to position it on a paper according to their 'preferred' place. The suggestion is given instruction to do this exercise spontaneously and playfully, according to the 'answers' which come to their mind in the moment.
- When all the clusters are on the paper, the client may additionally be asked to draw an image for each of them as they come spontaneously, using colours. The client is also told that if an image comes for a group of clusters (rather than for an individual cluster), to draw that image instead.
- When this process is completed, we ask the client to look at the whole picture and to share their experience about the whole process. We also ask the client what he sees in the picture and how he feels about the different elements of the picture. Many clients at this point create or relate verbal narratives, proper stories.

Thus the interpretation process is now additionally enriched with the inputs of the client's own psyche to the WAE data. An analyst could then check their own initial insights and hypotheses against these client inputs, safeguarding the interpretation process of the analyst's own projections and limitations (at least to certain extent). This is just one of the examples of how the living images of soul which the WAE surfaced could be mirrored back to the client with the invitation for personal engagement. It is essential to emphasise that, like with any other method used in analytic work, it is always a partnership between the analyst and a client and that any interpretation offered from an analyst is only food for thought for the client and serves only to stimulate the client's own understanding of and connection with their psyche. In this way, the client owns the results of the process, and their own communication with the unconscious is facilitated, which is always a goal of the analytic relationship. Where clients can participate in the interpretation process in this way, the insights and further developments prove to be of a deeply transformative nature.

The insights then emerge in an organic way and, in time, create a mosaic of meaning which can inform a multilayered interpretation process. The words from the WAE and the subsequent images will reoccur long after the WAE has been completed, in the creative and meaningful ways of the 'director of the unconscious', acting as guides on the client journey.

Bearing in mind that the WAE is used for different purposes (see Chapters 11 and 12), a whole spectrum of the usage of the results could be outlined. These can be based on drawing hypothetical conclusions only from an analyst's insights to collaborative interpretation with the client using the analyst as a sounding board. An analyst must be aware that the words, the images evoked by the WAE will 'work' with the client in any case and that the analytic relationship should hold the space for their transformative potential. They will accompany the client, closer to consciousness. Infant research describes this through the concept of the *evoked companion* (Stern 1985; see Chapter 9).

References

Lepori, D 2015, 'Introduction to WAE', [Seminar notes], C G Jung Institute, Zurich.
Stern, D 1985, *The Interpersonal World of the Infant: A View from Psychoanalysis and Developmental Psychology*, Basic Books, New York.

9 Behind words

Developmental perspective

Nada O'Brien

Behind words

Stern (1985) remarks that during the first few years the infant lives in memories of former interactions (so called representations of interactions which are generalised – RIGs), regardless of whether the caregiver is physically present or not. Even if the caregiver is present, the infant is actually at the same time also with a *regulating historical other* (or the image of the sum of interactional experiences). The time dimension of RIGs is complex: Stern feels that the infant has to deal both with its past, lived experience of togetherness with the caregiver, his subjective experience and, at the same time, the actual presence of the other. Thus, the *evoked companion* (p. 102) is present all the time, and both infants and adults are seldom (if ever) alone. It seems that we are all the time in a state of interaction, in a preverbal flow of amodal mental, affective and bodily sensations which knit the overall inner predisposition for each specific life experience and interaction (O'Brien 2018b). The evoked companion or historical other comprises personifications of RIGs, which are the building blocks of complexes (Jacoby 1999). Evoked companion comes with a dynamics of the deepest, most authentic self developed before words, casting historical other on the verbal self.

Development of the senses of self

From the perspective of infant research and psychoanalysis, the underlying dynamics of human life and maturation are portrayed in the formative period of the development of the self. The term 'self' is used in a developmental context signifying 'Supraordinate organisation responsible for regulating the system of the psyche. The centre of this organisation is the self or self-organisation' (Jacoby 1999, p. 48). Lichtemberg emphasised that the self is the 'independent center for initiating, organising and integrating experience and motivation' (Lichtenberg et al. 1992, p. 58).

Emergent self

During the first two months of life, the infant experiences events that become organised into more comprehensive structures. This is a development period of connecting single events based on inherent/archetypal and biographical 'logic'. Inherent/archetypal and biographical 'logic' is the remarkable manifestation of archetypes in action – universal organising principles which connect single experiences into universal forms which are observable in individual lives. Archetypes can be comprehended as formulae; underlying motion patterns manifest as typical behavioural patterns and automatic and unconscious reactions. 'The archetype itself is empty and purely formal, nothing but a *facultas praeformandi*, a possibility of representation which is given a priori. The representations themselves are not inherited, only the forms' (CW 9i, para. 155). The psyche's central archetype is the Self (different to the concepts of the self described in developmental psychology), and it is the archetype of meaning. Therefore, the first infant experiences at this earliest stage are beginning to be connected by the underlying principle of meaning, which is innate and universal.

Here, we are in a liminal space between archetypal, collective and universal – and developmental, individual and unique; a formative space of inherent potential and influences of the environment which model the matrices of personality. These matrices operate unconsciously and largely determine automatic human reactions, experiences, evaluations and behavioural patterns, permeating the entire human life as autonomous energy clusters with the tendency to be integrated into the conscious energy field (Ego). This results in the enlargement and enrichment of consciousness and releases creative potential. Jung empirically proved the existence and patterns of functioning of these energy clusters and termed them *complexes* (Escamilla 2021). On the developmental, biographical level of each individual, their origin is in the period of the emergent self, with the first blocks of memory, representations of interactions, which have been generalised (RIGs). RIGs are formed according to the infant's unique logic of evaluating experience and sense (Stern 1985). Arguably, this is the origin of the infant's subjective life. The emphasis here is on the *emergent* self – it is emerging into the world via the dual union with the mother and, ultimately, from the very 'source', the origin of life.

Core self

Around the second and third month, with the emergent self, the infant smile occurs, and the journey of experiencing *I* and *The Other* begins at a more differentiated level. RIGs, as 'islands of consistency' (Stern 1985, p. 14) form the sense of core self which brings the infant sense of *I*, of authorship of intentions and relationship with the regulative other. It is a flux of both core self vs. other and core self with other. These building blocks of relationship patterns are formed between the second and seventh months and remain an unconscious matrix of relatedness. The infant's sense of self depends on the other, the caregiver, especially in feeling safe. The development period of the core self is characterised by self-agency (control over self-generated action), self-coherence (having a sense of being a non-fragmented, physical whole), self-affectivity (patterned inner feelings) and self-history (continuity with one's past). Therefore, the core self is a more differentiated sense of *I* resulting from the interaction between the initial innate qualities of the infant with the environment.

The timing in which a caregiver reacts to the infant's needs and stimuli, the quality of resonance between the child and caregiver (form, content, intensity and the like), which developmental psychology and psychoanalysis recognise as different types of *attunement* (including misattunement), the spaciousness the infant is given for their expression, all these model future patterns of relatedness. This is especially true regarding relational expectations (based on the generalised experiences with the caregivers in these early stages), thus, connotatively, relational evaluation and quality. These all form an underlying individual *style* of relatedness. An illustrative analogy of this period could be a music *jam session*: Automatic ways a musician relates in spontaneous music communication (O'Brien 2018a).

Subjective self

This phase of the sense of self-development is marked by intersubjectivity, experienced and lived without words. Infants can share intention, the direction of focus and feeling states. This period marks a development of their personal styles of communication. Depending on the caregiver's attunement to the infant, the distribution of energy between the capacity for self-focus and engagement with the outside world is modelled, which remains an unconscious, automatic pattern of intersubjectivity throughout life. Furthermore, the implications of sharing intention, focus direction and feeling states are profound and multifold. The infant can be aware of the mother or caregiver's feeling state while focusing on the content of their communication. To the extent that they feel safe, a balance between managing the environment and their inner states and focusing on the object of attention is achieved. During this formative period, the ability to concentrate develops and becomes unconscious and automatic. Therefore, developmental (not inborn) introversion and extroversion preferences are powerfully predisposed in this way, because if the infant feels unsafe in the presence of a caregiver for example, due to a caregiver's inner states, which make them unfit to answer the infant's need and are not *good enough* (Winnicott 1957), the available energy will be mainly distributed to manage the *being with* (concerning the caregiver) rather than focusing on the shared object of attention in a balanced way. This can cause concentration and learning problems later on and, in extreme cases, a bipolar dynamic/disorder.

In this period, therefore, the infant forms the experience of what is sharable with the significant other, and thus a *non-sharable self* and *private self* are modelled. The *non-sharable self* becomes non-sharable even to the person themselves in later life; it is pushed into the unconscious, where it resides as a personal Shadow. However, it does not cease to exist, and it determines a person's automatic preferences and evaluations of life experience in the form of the *evoked other*.

The *private self* is accessible both to the person and potentially to trusted others (in certain conditions) but might not be expressible verbally. In this period, the *false self* (Winnicott 1960) is also apparent: 'Other people's expectations can become of overriding importance, overlaying or contradicting the original sense of self, the one connected to the very roots of one's being . . . through this false self, the infant builds up a false set of relationships, and by means of introjections even attains a show of being real'. The infant then provides attunement to the caregivers and lives a life of imitation without spontaneity. However, the role of the false self is vital in preventing something worse – hurting or destroying the true self, of which the extreme consequence would be a disintegration of *I*.

All these structures containing the infant's sense of self flow simultaneously and remain throughout one's life. All these non-verbal senses of self, all these dimensions of the deepest authentic identity, including the non-sharable self and private self, are evoked during the WAE. The deepest layers of the individual's sense of self, identity and modeled ways of being in life are, as described, essentially nonverbal but *coenesthetic* (O'Brien 2018b). Now, what happens with the sense of verbal self?

Verbal self

In the 15- to 18-month period, the infant's capacity to consider herself an object for her own reflection becomes apparent as language develops. There is an emergence of the *objective self* together with the *subjective self*. Words bring the naming of a child's experience and an accurate mirroring of the deepest layers of him/herself by the objective world. At the same time, words bring a split, either by being untrue to the child's experience and naming it falsely (often due to significant others mistaking a child for projections of their unconscious contents) or by the inability to name it at all. In the fairy tale 'Rumpelstiltskin' (Lepori 2020), discovering a true name releases healing or magical energy for new developments.

Furthermore, the 'devil' or 'lord of the underworld' is referred to as 'No-Named', cross-culturally reflecting the disallowed part of the self to exist in the "human world" (consciousness). This split brings the life-long dynamics of deep truth and betrayal, acceptance and rejection, shame and guilt, and it questions the acknowledgement of the *I am* experience. Again, an analogy can be drawn from the Bible (St John): 'In the beginning was the word'. Through it, the (external) world came into existence; it was an orientation for moving through life, as the Old Greek *herma* implied (phallus-shaped stones set on ancient crossroads personifying the presence of the god Hermes, protector of journeymen and words; hence the word *term*/terminology), orientation and guides of our thinking and being. Therefore, naming an infant's experience (or, in a pedagogical situation, the student's experience) must be an act of mirroring, not the imposition of a false meaning.

Behind words: Remembering Sophia

Words with complex indicators surface the developmental dynamics of the non-verbal and verbal senses of self. Furthermore, they feature the insights into the ancestral, cultural historical other and, ultimately, the archetypal unconscious source. They are pregnant with the lost light (*lumen naturae*) of Sophia.

> The ego does not create itself. The unconscious creates the ego but forgets it, or rather never knew it. This knowledge comes only when the ego reaches sufficient development that it can refuse to take the responsibility for everything in the psyche. At that point the ego is no longer identical with the psyche, the psyche becomes an objective reality and Divine Wisdom (Sophia) can awaken to awareness of Her existence. The ego has become a reflecting *mirror* for the emerging consciousness of the Self.
>
> (Edinger 1992, p. 133)

References

Edinger, E 1992, *Ego and Archetype*, Shambala, Boulder.
Jacoby, M 1999, *Jungian Psychotherapy & Contemporary Infant Research*, Routledge, London.
Jung, CG 1934/1955, *The Archetypes and the Collective Unconscious*, CW 9i.
Jung, CG 2000, *The Collected Works of C. G. Jung* (CW), Princeton University Press, Princeton.
Lepori, D 2020, 'Rumpelstiltskin: Archetypal view on ethics', In N O'Brien & J O'Brien (Eds.), *Professional Practice of Jungian Coaching*, pp. 205–212, Routledge, London.
Lichtenberg, J, Lachmann, F, Fosshage J 1992, *Self and Motivational Systems*, Hillsdale Publishing, Hillsdale.
O'Brien, N 2018a, *Music and the Unconscious*, Dosije Studio, Belgrade.
O'Brien, N 2018b, 'Who is listening? A psychoanalytic view on listening phenomena', *New Sound*, vol. 52, pp. 131–147. Visited February 12, 2024, <doi: 10.5937/newso18521310>.
O'Brien, N 2023, 'Deep music pedagogy and four ways of being', *Studies in Teaching and Education*, vol. 72, no. 2, pp. 185–196.
Stern, D 1985, *The Interpersonal World of the Infant: A View from Psychoanalysis and Developmental Psychology*, Basic Books, New York.
Winnicott, D 1957, *The Child, the Family, and the Outside World*, Penguin, London.
Winnicott, D 1960, 'Ego distortion in terms of true and false self', In *The Maturational Process and the Facilitating Environment: Studies in the Theory of Emotional Development*, International Universities Press, New York, pp. 140–157.

10 WAE examination document
Example

Nada O'Brien

When providing presentations for the WAE, written consent must be obtained from the patient, and care taken to protect patient anonymity. Information by which the patient might be identified may not be included.

'Title'

Examiner:

Candidate:

Year

Table of contents

1 **Anamnesis**
2 **Description of the experimental setting, initial counter-transference**
3 **Analysis of the feedback after the first part of the experiment and Data from the unconscious**
4 **Analysis of Protocol**

   Tables and graphs
   Prolonged response times
   Analysis by complex indicators
   Qualitative analysis of responses
   Response reactions and thoughts about perseveration

5 **Context interview**
6 **Interpretation Hypothesis**

   Map of Complexes
   Synopsis of the main findings

7 **Indications for further therapeutic work**
8 **Reflections on the WAE experience for the candidate's individuation process**

   Candidate's own complexes

DOI: 10.4324/9781032716572-10

Appendix: Borderline personality disorder short description and symptoms References

Anamnesis

Client identifying code: D
Gender: Female
Age: 44

Parents and carers

D's mother was born in 1952 in a poor part of Europe, the younger of two sisters by three years. She committed suicide when D was in her 20s.

D's father was born in 1944. He had a son from his first marriage. D was the only child of his second marriage. He worked as a solicitor.

Position in birth order (when there are siblings)

D has a half-brother who is 11 years older than her. They had a close relationship.

Ancestors

D's maternal grandmother (MGM) did not provide adequate food and clothing for D's mother.

D spoke with affection about her paternal grandmother (PGM), who she described as a kind woman.

D did not speak about her paternal grandparents. D mentioned that there was always a conflict between her parents about their respective origin – urban ('civilised, with manners') paternal grandparents vs. rural ('primitive') maternal grandparents.

Stories or knowledge about birth circumstances and early childhood

Although she reports no complications with her birth, her mother found it impossible to breastfeed her. She suffered from depression. On reflection, D feels that she had been a burden on her mother.

Childhood and youth

D's earliest memories are of walks with her mother to bookstores and shops, but the mother never wanted to buy anything for D. D wore clothes of other children in the family. D remembers her father as always very strict, she never knew in what mood he would be. He always shouted. Her first memory of him was him bringing home a little fox he found while hunting. She loved animals from her early childhood to date. D was quite sick as a child (chicken pox, pneumonia), and she remembers her father reading to her. He was rarely warm, but it felt nice when he was. D remembers that her parents quarreled a lot throughout her childhood.

Due to her parents' constant quarrels, when D was 12, she went to an institution for children without parental care on her own and asked to be admitted. She was not admitted, and her parents divorced soon after. D's half brother and her father also quarreled a lot, and quarrels are the most present theme in her childhood. When the father forbade her brother to study movie production (what he really wanted) the brother started drinking and remained alcoholic for the rest of his life. D remembers her half-brother as rebellious, always saying openly what he meant, down to earth. Both father and brother loved animals, but her mother did not like them. Both mother and father constantly compared her with other children from their sides of the family, and they were always better than her in everything. (After her mother left, she terminated any contact a contact with wider family members.)

When D was about to finish high school, her mother arranged for her to go to teacher training college, and her father entered her for law school. D ran away from home and enrolled in veterinary science. Nothing she or her brother did was good enough for her father. When D was 18 her mother left to live in Germany, and at that moment D bought her first dog. Since then, she has always had animals. After a few years she decided to marry her boyfriend but then ran away from her own wedding – to Germany. By that time, her mother was very ill with rheumatism and had suffered 11 surgeries. D worked as an air hostess stewardess, traveling a lot.

Social context and climate (for example, born in a period of war)

D was born in a middle-low-income country in a climate of social conflict. She migrated to a West European country when she was 18, and when she was in her 20s, war broke out. Her brother fought in the war and suffered undiagnosed severe PTSD. She managed her life to make it possible for him to visit her for long periods of convalescence.

Education

D is a highly educated person, well-read very curious about different topics She has a post graduate university degree in photography and related subjects.

Economic circumstances

D had been working as a stewardess while supporting herself and her sick mother. At 39 years old D was diagnosed with breast cancer. She had to stop working while going through her medical treatment. D then returned to her home country and struggled to find a steady job. She worked for few years in different jobs and she would suddenly change them even if they were interesting for her. D did not seem to be very rational with managing her finances and left an impression of always struggling financially. She would make sudden decisions which would affect her financial stability.

Occupations and interests

D worked as a stewardess, then as a project manager in an large organisation embassy and at present she is a project manager in an organisation supporting children. She has been engaged with dogs (exhibitions, breeding, care) all her life. She enjoys making photographic and film documentaries.

Significant events

While D was employed as a stewardess, she worked three shifts, supporting both herself and her mother and two friends who ran away from her native country, which at that time was in a state of war. D visited her father who got ill and he soon died.

She fell in love with a person whom her mother did not trust. She kept saying he wanted to marry D because of her status in Germany. Eventually, her mother's views proved to be correct, and he soon left D. A few years later she met an Englishman whom she loved most in her life and had a great time together for 2 years. He had a girlfriend in England, was honest about that, and they kept spending weekends together traveling to different places. At one point D realised that she loved him so much that she could not continue unless the relationship was exclusive, and she decided not to see him ever again. Since then she did not have a serious relationship.

A few years after, D's best friend, who was visiting, found D's mother dead. She had committed suicide by hanging. D returned to her native country, lived as a sub-tenant and sold nuts on the market to survive. A year after that D's brother died of a stroke. That is when she found a job as a project manager.

Present family and circumstances

Four years ago D had breast cancer diagnosed and went through difficult surgery and tough treatment. She is now the project manager of an international organisation caring for children with challenging backgrounds and is finishing her studies (film production). She is making documentaries and enjoys it a great deal. She is still under a heavy hormonal therapy and has put on a lot of weight due to the treatment, and she is bothered about it. D has two dogs and a cat, and her dog has been winning trophies at the exhibitions till recently, when D decided to stop doing this and let her dog be just playful. D does not have children. She said that she did get pregnant with the first boyfriend. Her mother had said that D will have her baby 'over her dead body'.

Significant problems

Except for her illness, D herself did not report any significant problems. She mentioned only that sometimes she gets very angry and that sometimes she feels very sad and lonely.

Pervasive themes

Quarrels, conflicts, extreme situations, apparently opposite topics 'see-saw' (such as very spiritual topics and then primal dramas like exploration of dog fights), always something marked with drama and intensity and also broken continuity.

Expectations about the WAE

D was very excited about going through the WAE process and she was very curious about the experiment. She said that she was hopeful that it might bring her peace.

Description of the experimental setting, initial counter-transference

Experimental setting

The experiment was conducted in a therapy room where I work with clients. D was familiar with the space since she was participating in a developmental programme designed for her team. D came to the meeting looking forward to the experience and saying that she 'adores' those kinds of activities. Before we started, D forwarded a comment in a witty way: 'God knows what will you think of me after this and I will probably end up in an institution!' and she laughed.

I used the 50-word list. I used printed sheets of the stimulus words, arranged in two pages of groups of 25 words for my easy reading. The pages were clipped inside an A4 notebook, and I marked responses with a pencil. The responses were subsequently transferred to electronic format. Once we were comfortably seated I explained the approach, using the following format:

We will now begin the Word Association Experiment.
  I will read out a list of 50 words, separately, one after another. After hearing each word, please answer, as quickly as possible, with the very first that comes to mind after hearing the word I call out. If possible, please answer with one word only. I will measure the time you take to answer on the stopwatch and write down your responses. Do you have any questions?

D did not have any questions and was ready to start. She was focused and responsive. I measured the reaction times from when the first vowel of the first accentuated syllable was pronounced to the end of the word. Response times were noted in hundredths of a second. (I subsequently converted these to one-fifths of a second by Excel formula then rounded up or down manually to the nearest whole one-fifth of a second. I repeated this exercise before the calculation of the probable mean to check accuracy.) I carefully observed the client from the periphery of my vision during the session and noted complex indicators.

After the first round of the 50 words, we had a 20-minute break. I kindly invited D to give her comments about her experience so far. D expressed in a witty manner her inability to give associations about marriage. '*Why is it so difficult for me?*' She asked this several times as a rhetorical question. Then she had to make a phone call to a young man who kept phoning her during the first part of the experiment (she noticed that in the break) – a person without parents, a heroin addict a few weeks out from the institution where he was detoxicated and went through the abstinence crisis. He wanted to move to a different city and start living 'his own life' in his way, redefining his relationships with the organisation D works for. Later she commented that the young man and her concern for him reminded her a lot of her brother who died.

At the beginning of the second trial I gave the following instructions:

We will repeat the experiment in order to see what you were able to remember. The time will not be measured. It does not matter if you cannot remember the word you said during the first session. If a new word comes to mind instead of the first word, just say it.

Initial counter-transference

When D came, she was energised; she commented that she was looking forward to doing this activity. I immediately felt energised as well and as if there was a flow that started carrying me also. It could be described with words like: 'Ok, now we are going to do it, it is time'. I was aware of the change in me and found it curious.

My reactions and feelings regarding D during the WAE were:

Pain/sadness I felt in my heart and solar plexus (especially with the words 'sick', 'fight', 'pray' and 'home'). With the word 'marry I felt (somehow spatially) *a void* – an empty space stretching from left to right and then a little something at the bottom right appearing; I felt worry, fear (almost upset). Throughout the experiment I felt warmth towards her and empathy. I found myself admiring her spiritedness.

Analysis of the feedback after the first part of the experiment and data from the unconscious

After the experiment D commented that the WAE seemed to be quite a deep and complex thing because she was surprised about words inspiring different reactions. In a witty manner she repeated her surprise about failing to give associations to the 'Marry' word: 'I am still pondering about my incapability to associate to "marry" word. Why? I must be definitely a nutter! Interesting!' We agreed the date of the next session, for a week ahead, and concluded the meeting. D went home apparently cheerful.

SW 'marry' provoked indeed the highest number of complex indicators (six), and it is the only word entailed with such a high number in the whole word list. This fact could indicate a multilevel importance of meanings that this issue carries, vital for D's psyche. As if this very word attracts more than one complex to be projected on the rich semantics it brings. At this point, without going into interpretation, it provokes a thought that it could present more than 'just' a complex. What that 'more' could be is not clear yet and remains to be gradually discovered observing the mosaic of the whole. It also strikes me that there might be libido around *marrying* opposites, a unifying symbol bringing transformation into D's life. This thought became especially present after the two dreams D reported:

Both parts of the WAE were accompanied with dreams.
I return home, unlock the entrance door and hear my dog Bri (this is short for Britannia) pocking the door with her paw. I am confused because I know I left her in her cage when I left home. The dogs are very happy to see me. I look at the cage and for the first time I see the door on the cage that Bri opened and got out from the cage.

My friend visits me and I see that her entire legs are covered with cuts – as if somebody was inscribing x/o game with a knife. The scars are black, no blood. One scar is very big and open and I stare at it and see only black inside. I am flabbergasted because she does not react to the scars and I wonder where the bone is and where is the tissue in the scar.

D's comments:

Bri is the most wonderful creature in the world. I adore her. I remember clearly that I was not angry at her but happy how smart she was to find her way out.
My friend had a very difficult life, she is a true fighter. X-O is a game that takes me back to my childhood . . .

When I take into consideration my initial counter-transference and these dreams I wonder whether D was 'ready' to start dealing with her pain and woundedness – as if there was a decision made . . . Thus the flow of energy that 'infected' me as well at the beginning of the experiment? I was also thankful for the good ally in the helpful curiosity with clear, motivating and soothing presence of spirit in her wittiness and humor.

Analysis of protocol

Template

Word number	Stimulus word	Reaction time 5ths	Reaction time Sec.	Reaction	Reproduction	Reaction notes	Complex Indicator Types — Over PM	Re	sounds	other	CIs	Response Type — Factual	Egocentric
1	Play	8.5	1.7	alley	+								√
2	mouth	9.5	1.9	word	+							√	
3	Free	49	9.8	happiness	open sea*	tone of voice	T				3		√
4	Car	18	3.6	end	+	tone of voice					1		√
5	make	8.5	1.7	chaos	shit						1		√
6	friend	9	1.8	V	+	tone of voice					1		√
7	stupid	9.5	1.9	happy	fool						1		√
8	together	14	2.7	sharing	+	tone of voice					1		√
9	Go	30	5.9	far	+	tone of voice	T				2		√
10	habit	49	9.7	monotony	boredom		T				2		√
11	New	18	3.6	challenge	experience					st	2		√
12	Tree	12	2.3	stalk	+							√	
13	Kiss	16	3.1	"sljap"	+	it is watery, wet, hated it when I was little				MW, b, l	3		√
14	finger	7	1.4	direction	+								
15	Sad	22	4.4	unaware	alone	tone of voice	T			b	4		√
16	knife	19	3.7	pain	anatomy		T				2		√
17	dance	18	3.5	hall	+								
18	choice	16	3.2	problem	bravery					st	2		√
19	naked	34	6.8	happy	free		T			st	3		√
20	Plain	12	2.4	clever	cheek						1		√
21	Learn	19	3.8	freedom	richness		T			st	3		√
22	Pity	14	2.7	stupidity	+					st	1		√
23	weak	19	3.7	ignorant	not stupid but ignorant		T			b, MW, st	5		√
24	Boss	39	7.8	anarchy	+		T				1		√
25	Wait	16	3.2	hope	losing time	tone of voice				MW	3		√
26	family	28	5.6	beehive	voice		T				2		√

(Continued)

(Continued)

Word number	Stimulus word	Reaction time 5ths	Reaction time Sec.	Reaction	Reproduction	Reaction notes	Over PM	Re	sounds	other	CIs	Factual	Egocentric
27	Sick	55	11	brave	alone		T			b, st	4		✓
28	Cat	22	4.3	play	+		T				1		✓
29	Pray	30	5.9	desperate	weakness		T		✓	b	3		✓
30	wages	17	3.4	merit	+								
31	Old	17	3.3	quality	experience					st	2		✓
32	fight	33	6.5	bravery	Titanic	tone of voice				st	4		✓
33	glass	22	4.4	bottom	+		T				1	✓	
34	marry	98	19.5	cage	don't know		T	✓		b, l, MW	6		✓
35	guilt	25	4.9	mistake	+		T				1		✓
36	work	17	3.4	must	obligation						1		✓
37	proud	24	4.7	brave	+		T			st	2		✓
38	fear	18	3.5	stupidity	flying					st	2		✓
39	red	17	3.3	black	+								
40	water	12	2.4	depth	open sea						1	✓	
41	hurt	23	4.6	to be selfish	to be stupid		T		✓	b, MW, st	5		✓
42	flower	35	7	that hippie sign	+		T			MW	2		✓
43	evil	22	4.3	anger	man - as human being		T			b, MW	4		✓
44	party	31	6.1	boredom	+		T				1		✓
45	fly	12	2.4	fear	+								✓
46	death	17	3.3	inevitability	+								✓
47	clean	23	4.6	FALSE	problem		T				2		✓
48	try	17	3.4	know	to be brave					MW, st	3		✓
49	sin	21	4.1	experience	+		T			st	2		✓
50	home	18	3.5	tweed	+	tone of voice					1		[:/]
	MEDIAN	18	3.6										
				are over 18									

Graph 1: Reaction time

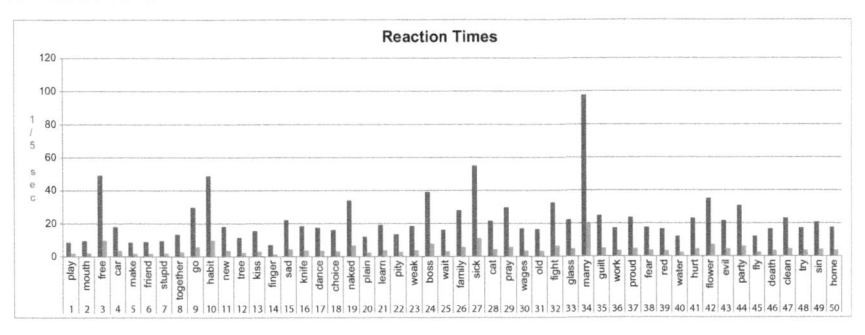

[Reaction Times bar chart, 1/5 sec, stimuli 1–50]

Graph 2: Complex indicators

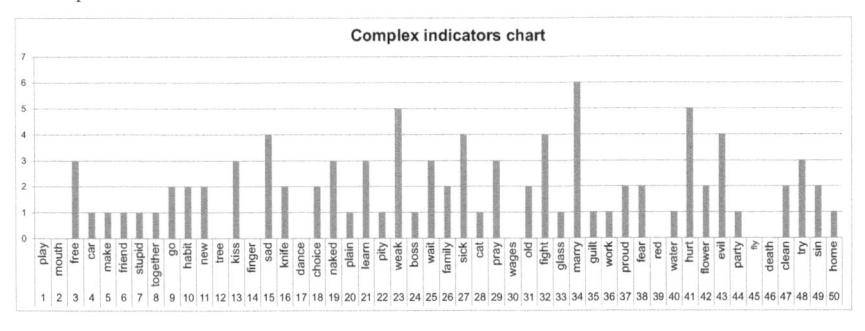

[Complex indicators chart, stimuli 1–50]

Prolonged response times

Responses were measured in 1/5th of a second. Prolonged response times are deemed those above the probable mean (median). The probable mean for the whole test was 18 fifths, which is somewhat longer than the average 9–14 fifths (Kast). This is the list of PRTs given in ascending order of response times.

16	knife	19	3.7	pain	anatomy
21	learn	19	3.8	freedom	richness
23	weak	19	3.7	ignorant	Not stupid but ignorant
49	sin	21	4.1	experience	+
15	sad	22	4.4	unaware	alone
28	cat	22	4.3	play	+
33	glass	22	4.4	bottom	+
43	evil	22	4.3	anger	man – as human being
47	clean	23	4.6	false	problem
41	hurt	23	4.6	to be selfish	to be stupid
37	proud	24	4.7	brave	+
35	guilt	25	4.9	mistake	+
26	family	28	5.6	beehive	voice
9	go	30	5.9	far	+
29	pray	30	5.9	desperate	weakness
44	party	31	6.1	boredom	+
32	fight	33	6.5	bravery	Titans
19	naked	34	6.8	happy	free

(*Continued*)

(Continued)

42	flower	35	7	that hippie sign	+
24	boss	39	7.8	anarchy	+
3	free	49	9.8	happiness	open sea
10	habit	49	9.7	monotony	boredom
27	sick	55	11	brave	alone
34	marry	98	19.5	cage	don't know

There are noticeably short response times in the first third of the word list (showed next in the context of the surrounding words):

1	play	8.5	1.7	alley	+
2	mouth	9.5	1.9s	word	+
3	*free*	*49*	*9.8*	*happiness*	*open sea**
4	*car*	*18*	*3.6*	*end*	+
5	*make*	*8.5*	*1.7*	*chaos*	shit
6	*friend*	*9*	*1.8*	*V*	+
7	*stupid*	*9.5*	*1.9*	*happy*	fool
8	together	14	2.7	sharing	+
9	go	30	5.9	far	+
10	habit	49	9.7	monotony	boredom
11	new	18	3.6	challenge	experience
12	tree	12	2.3	stalk	+
13	kiss	16	3.1	"sljap"	+
14	*finger*	*7*	*1.4*	*direction*	+

These very short response times might indicate a defensive reaction (or something else of relevance). I had in mind D's comments when she came to do the experiment showing concern for how I would value her performance, in terms of her 'success' in the experiment. This prompted me to think that the very low reaction times of the first two SWs are actually showing D's tension and stress and that later on that she was perhaps more concerned with the semantics. I would be inclined to consider these low reaction times indicating emotionally charged reactions showing rather D's anxiety prior to the WAE than relating to the semantics of the first two SWs. This noted, I would consider the reaction times closer to the median as reactions without CIs related to time (12–18).

Analysis by complex indicators

There are eight types of responses to SW:

1	Repetition of SW	1
2	Laughter	2
3	Body movements	8
4	Multiple word re	8
5	Tone of voice	9
6	Stereotypes	14
7	Prolonged time	24
8	False reproductions	26

There were 12 words with three or more complex indicators:

13	Kiss	16	3.1	'sljap'	+ It is watery, wet, hated it	b, l, MW	3
15	Sad	22	4.4	unaware	Alone	tone of voice	4
19	Naked	34	6.8	happy	free	st	3
21	Learn	19	3.8	freedom	richness	st	3
23	Weak	19	3.7	ignorant	not stupid but ignorant	b, MW, st	5
25	Wait	16	3.2	hope	loosing time	tone of voice, MW	3
27	Sick	55	11	brave	alone	b, st	4
29	Pray	30	5.9	desperate	weakness	b	3
32	Fight	33	6.5	bravery	Titans	b, tone of voice, st	5
34	Marry	98	19.5	cage	don't know	b, l, MW, r	6
41	Hurt	23	4.6	to be selfish	to be stupid	b, MW, st	5
43	Evil	22	4.3	anger	man as human	b, MW	4
48	Try	17	3.4	know	to be brave	MW, st	3

Tone of voice

In quite a few RWs there was a very specific change in D's tone of voice. It got deeper, slightly dramatic in a more quiet manner condensed with emotion, attracting the attention. It would strike me that every time this change happened I would feel a sense of something potentially dramatic. It made me more alert in a way of anticipating something serious. It also made me feel it was something private, her secret. Because it appeared to be a particular response style, occurring frequently, I could not disregard it, and I marked it as a complex indicator.

Stereotypes

Using the word stems happy, free, experience, brave, stupid, the following stereotypes were noted:

HAPPY[1]

3	free	49	9.8	happiness	open sea*	tone of voice
7	stupid	9.5	1.9	happy	fool	
19	naked	34	6.8	happy	free	

FREE

| 19 | naked | 34 | 6.8 | happy | free |
| 21 | learn | 19 | 3.8 | freedom | richness |

Observing the reactions to SWs 'free' and 'happy' I noticed three lines of interpretation:
Free-Happy-Naked-Open Sea

Happy-Stupid-Fool
Learn-Freedom-Richness

It occurs to me that these three lines could indicate a potential path for diagnostics and also a potential therapeutic approach. Having in mind D's own definition of freedom (to be herself) and the archetypal landscape in elemental form of the *open sea* I got an image of the freedom and happiness for D is the connection to the Self, the individuation journey and the free access and contact to the unconscious (see Context interview). Given the importance that these words have in the WAE, I am also thinking about the current cathexis of her psyche.

Echo of the inhibiting qualities of her parental figures' personalities, childhood experiences, tragedies, painful and 'negative' contents could be condensed in the Stupid-Happy-Fool. It is stupid to go along the first line illustrated above; only fools do that.

Where her psyche shows an opening in this moment is through her ability to learn. It gives her energy and potentially fulfills her.

Dynamically, I see expanding tendency in the first line (open sea), limiting counter-tendency in the second and full-filling (the third dimension of depth?) in the third – *tertium non datur?*

EXPERIENCE

11	new	18	3.6	challenge	experience		1
49	sin	21	4.1	experience	+		2
31	old	17	3.3	quality	experience		2

Dual connotation seen in the first three stereotypes seem to occur with the word 'experience' as well. Meeting something new, different to the known pattern is providing an experience. Openness to try. No matter whether it will be 'right' or 'wrong' – 'sin' is an experience as well. And experiences build up in time and potentially draw a life wisdom and quality. It might be 'a sin' to try, as well . . . (expanding – limiting).

BRAVE

18	choice	16	3.2	problem	bravery		2
27	sick	55	11	brave	alone		4
32	fight	33	6.5	bravery	Titans	T, tov,	5
37	proud	24	4.7	brave	+		2
48	try	17	3.4	know	to be brave		3

Taking into consideration that it was 'sick' SW and 'brave' as a response that triggered D to reveal that she suffered from cancer and went through a tough surgery and very difficult treatment and her emphasis that she went through this alone gives special weight to her responses 'proud', 'try' and 'know'. I am thinking of a hero in fairy tales that has to go through tough experiences to learn what he is made of, who he is and what powers he possesses. The kingship seems to be a lot in this 'knowing'. Try-Know-To be brave shed special light on 'learn' and 'richness' touched earlier, raising awareness of how much strength and bravery it takes to *try* penetrating the boundary of known safe old mechanisms . . . D's words ring here: 'I was thinking not to do anything when I learned that I have cancer. Could not imagine myself going through that awful medical process without any assurance and support . . . I was so tired of pain. It took me a long while to make a decision to try . . . This is why I felt I could say yes to this painful work with children. I do understand them and I can meet their pain'.

STUPID

22	pity	14	2.7	stupidity	+	
23	weak	19	3.7	ignorant	not stupid but ignorant	
38	fear	18	3.5	stupidity	flying	
41	hurt	23	4.6	to be selfish	to be stupid	body movements

Not either or, but both (Jung 1968, p. 143) . . . Jung's words come to mind. 'I feel that if I stop I will get ill . . . I have to keep on moving'. Could 'pity' be understood as potential danger of stopping? In such extraordinary survival situations (illness, mother's suicide, homeless, war . . .) when she 'had to' keep on moving? Thus the presence of one of the strongest tokens of censoring such action (bearing the father's image and her husband's later on): 'Stupid'. A fairy-tale image of whipping a princess (Anima) to limit her – keep her under control but not so strong to disable her to fly came to mind. Also how the forces that seem to be the worst enemies could be lifesaving sometimes. Therefore this 'stupid' attitude towards 'pity' could be understood as a defense against moving on, trying and fighting for her life. Fear-stupid-flying, again dualistic perspective: Does D 'know' that staying away from the pain, ground, reality, mother[2] is a way of escape (or running away)? At the same time it could echo her parents' censorship of her imagination and spirituality. The challenge is reaching the point where it would be safe to pity – have compassion with the wounds she bravely carries and that for the time being are presented through her friend . . . in the dream after the first part of the WAE. One fact we do know: She came to the stage. And again a hint of the potential approach from D's unconscious in the Weak-Ignorant-Not stupid but ignorant. Jung's words *'The biggest evil is non-awareness . . .'* (CW 11, p. 197) come to mind. It seems that 'try', 'learn', 'brave' are related to this, resulting with the understanding that she was not the actual reason for people calling her stupid but that they were not feeling ok (see Context interview).

Qualitative analysis of responses

Egocentric responses are marked when the client mentions a personal experience in response to the stimulus word (Kast 1980). In this context I read the egocentric responses as responses relating to the client's experience rather than responses which could be considered factual. There were some grey-zone responses, which I marked as egocentric in that they appeared to relate to the clients experience:

8	together	sharing	+
14	finger	direction	+
30	wages	merit	+
40	water	depth	open sea

Although these RWs could prompt us to think of some common colloquial associations, there was this delicate change in the tone of D's voice that I took as an indication that there was a personal experience colouring the reaction. There were five factual responses and 45 egocentric responses.

Given that the proportion of egocentric to factual reactions was high, according to Kast's classifications, I considered whether a dominating complex was constellated during the whole session, whether the client was predicate type, simple egocentric or an evaluating type. I concluded that the client was not a factual type. Given the fact that more than 50% of the responses were internal associations, I considered her to be an evaluating type. At the same time dominant complexes were constellated during the session. I am more inclined towards determining D as a constellation type, especially taking into account her dreams, comments, context, my counter-transference and relation between dominating complexes aroused during the WAE in relation to the dramatic history of D. Her strong evaluative style prompts me to think of D as most probably a dominant feeling type. Furthermore, her judgemental reactions to the behaviour that could be a feature of the dominant thinking type (for example her description of her brother) could indicate a reaction to her inferior function.

Response reactions and thoughts about perseveration

The way the response reactions seem to be arranged is striking: The reactions to the SW with complex indicators are grouped in larger clusters covering the whole word list, with sets of only one or two words in between which responses are without complex indicators. It is perhaps indicative that only in those 'intermediate' SWs we find those very few factual type responses in the entire experiment.

1	play	8.5	1.7	alley	+			
2	mouth	9.5	1.9	word	+ (factual)			
3	free	49	9.8	happiness	open sea*	tone of voice	T	2
4	car	18	3.6	end	+	tone of voice		1
5	make	8.5	1.7	chaos	shit			1
6	friend	9	1.8	V	+	tone of voice		1
7	stupid	9.5	1.9	happy	fool			1
8	together	14	2.7	sharing	+	tone of voice		1
9	go	30	5.9	far	+	tone of voice	T	2
10	habit	49	9.7	monotony	boredom		T	2
11	new	18	3.6	challenge	experience			1
12	tree	12	2.3	stalk	+ (factual)			
13	kiss	16	3.1	"sljap"	+	it is watery, wet, hated it when I was little		3
14	finger	7	1.4	direction	+			
15	sad	22	4.4	unaware	alone	tone of voice	T	4
16	knife	19	3.7	pain	anatomy		T	2
17	dance	18	3.5	hall	+ (factual)			
18	choice	16	3.2	problem	bravery			1
19	naked	34	6.8	happy	free		T	4
20	plain	12	2.4	clever	cheek			1
21	learn	19	3.8	freedom	richness		T	4
22	pity	14	2.7	stupidity	+			1
23	weak	19	3.7	ignorant	not stupid but ignorant		T	5
24	boss	39	7.8	anarchy	+		T	1
25	wait	16	3.2	hope	losing time	tone of voice	T	3
26	family	28	5.6	beehive	voice			2
27	sick	55	11	brave	alone	body movements	T	4
28	cat	22	4.3	play	+		T	1
29	pray	30	5.9	desperate	weakness		T	3
30	wages	17	3.4	merit	+			
31	old	17	3.3	quality	experience			1
32	fight	33	6.5	bravery	Titans	tone of voice	T	5
33	glass	22	4.4	bottom	+		T	1
34	marry	98	19.5	cage	don't know		T	6
35	guilt	25	4.9	mistake	+		T	1
36	work	17	3.4	must	obligation			1
37	proud	24	4.7	brave	+		T	2
38	fear	18	3.5	stupidity	flying			2
39	red		17	3.3	black	+ (factual)		
40	water		12	2.4	depth	open sea		
41	hurt	23	4.6	to be selfish	to be stupid	body movements	T	4
42	flower	35	7	that hippie sign	+		T	2
43	evil	22	4.3	anger	man - as huma nbeing	body movements	T	4
44	party	31	6.1	boredom	+		T	1

(Continued)

(Continued)

45	fly	12	2.4	fear	+			
46	death	17	3.3	inevitability	+			
47	clean	23	4.6	false	problem		T	2
48	try	17	3.4	know	to be brave			3
49	sin	21	4.1	experience	+		T	2
50	home	18	3.5	tweed	+	tone of voice		1

Perseverations and recovery time

3	free	49	9.8	happiness	open sea*	tone of voice	T	3
4	car	18	3.6	end	+	tone of voice		1
5	make	8.5	1.7	chaos	shit			1
6	friend	9	1.8	V	+	tone of voice		1
7	stupid	9.5	1.9	happy	fool			1
8	together	14	2.7	sharing	+	tone of voice		1
9	go	30	5.9	far	+	tone of voice	T	2
10	habit	49	9.7	monotony	boredom		T	2
11	new	18	3.6	challenge	experience	st		1
12	tree	12	2.3	stalk	+			

Observing this first cluster I noticed that the first SW 'free' (that is also recognised as a stereotype) has the highest number of complex indicators (T, tone of voice, incorrect reproduction) in the cluster and the highest prolonged response time (9.8). The following eight words in the cluster are all with the same type of complex indicators, varying in number. This observation led me to think about perseveration in the sense that the following words were echoing the emotion of the first SW ('free' – perseveration trigger) in the cluster. Perseveration is understood as 'echo of the emotion produced by a stimulus-word which continue to manifest in the next reactions, either via a related reaction or by prolonged reaction-time' (Lepori 2015). D's time reactions in this cluster are interesting in the sense that after a high prolonged time reaction SW (49) follows one that is of median value (18), and then the times that follow in the next three SWs are significantly low (8.5, 9, 9.5), indicating a contrast at the other end of time reactions. In this context, these reactions could also indicate an emotionally charged response, potentially a defense reaction. Regarding the recovery time it is rather rapid and drastic 49–18–8.5 than gradual, which might prompt a question whether it could be considered 'recovery time'. Or is it still perseveration ending with a reaction that is of more average value closer to median (14)?

3	free	49	9.8	happiness	open sea*	tone of voice	T	3
4	car	18	3.6	end	+	tone of voice		1
5	make	8.5	1.7	chaos	shit			1
6	friend	9	1.8	V	+	tone of voice		1
7	stupid	9.5	1.9	happy	fool			1
8	together	14	2.7	sharing	+	tone of voice		1

Given the definition that D gives in the Context regarding the word 'free': '*Freedom is when you are who you are and somebody either loves you or not. To be who you are is freedom for me*', as if D sets the essential dynamic at the very beginning in a nutshell, as a prologue in Shakespeare dramas. The way of driving her life stopped, and there is no way made further. There is a notion of chaos as a connotation of making. V is her best friend who was there for her in the most dramatic times of D's life, and it was V who found D's mother dead, having committed suicide. It is 'stupid' wanting to be happy and being stupid was quite a common censorship of D's natural sparkle of life within echoing reactions of her parents and partners later in D's life. Does this cluster actually show a constellation around the central issue of being herself? Marking the allies and 'enemies' on her individuation journey? I am understanding D's definition in a multidimensional way:

Developmentally – it seems from D's anamnesis and Context interview that she had more inhibitors than support in regards to her 'being herself' and developing her genuine potential.
Transgenerational
Cultural
Archetypal centered 're-ligare', with the Self and problems to discover her powers as in fairytales . . .

13	kiss	16	3.1	'sljap'	+	it is watery, wet, hated it when I waslittle		3
14	finger	7	1.4	direction	+			
15	sad	22	4.4	unaware	alone	tone of voice	T	4
16	knife	19	3.7	pain	anatomy		T	2
17	dance	18	3.5	hall	+ (factual)			

This cluster of reactions with complex indicators could be formed around the issue of connecting ('kiss'). Then there seem to be an ordering implication in the finger-direction (reflecting on D's parents' demand that she behaves the way they wanted). I wonder is there an empathy with the mother in the reactions sad-unaware-alone, D's actual deep resonance (and mirroring) with her mother that also resulted in living life the way she did (illness, sadness, loneliness . . .) also in relation to another way of aggression (but with different semantics): Knife-pain-anatomy?

18	choice	16	3.2	problem	bravery			1
19	naked	34	6.8	happy	free		T	4
20	plain	12	2.4	clever	cheak			1
21	learn	19	3.8	freedom	richness		T	4
22	pity	14	2.7	stupidity	+			1
23	weak	19	3.7	ignorant	not stupid but ignorant		T	5
24	boss	39	7.8	anarchy	+		T	1
25	wait	16	3.2	hope	losing time	tone of voice		3
26	family	28	5.6	beehive	voice		T	2
27	sick	55	11	brave	alone		T	4
28	cat	22	4.3	play	+		T	1
29	pray	30	5.9	desperate	weakness	body movements	T	3
30	wages	17	3.4	merit	+			

In addition to what was said earlier about the responses in this cluster I would like to focus the attention to the SW 'cat' especially in the context of the surrounding words:

27	sick	55	11	brave	alone		T	4
28	cat	22	4.3	play	+		T	1
29	pray	30	5.9	desperate	weakness	body movements	T	3
30	wages	17	3.4	merit	+			

The word 'cat' comes between two SWs of the survival importance for D: 'Sick' and 'Pray' (given her reflections, Context, anamnesis . . .). If we take into consideration the multilayered semantic weight of the cat symbol (*Retrieving the Sacred Feminine*, for example, or 'The Cat' by Von Franz) or 'just' perhaps the hardest achievable goal for D: To play safely, with support and approval, there might be an indication of her deepest fear and need. Observing these four SWs and types of reactions there might be enough indicators for perseveration, with the SW 'sick' being the perseveration trigger.

31	old	17	3.3	quality	experience			1
32	fight	33	6.5	bravery	Titans	tone of voice	T	5
33	glass	22	4.4	bottom	+		T	1
34	marry	98	19.5	cage	don't know		T	6
35	guilt	25	4.9	mistake	+		T	1
36	work	17	3.4	must	obligation			1
37	proud	24	4.7	brave	+		T	2
38	fear	18	3.5	stupidity	flying			2
39	*red*	*17*	*3.3*	*black*	*+ (factual)*			
40	*water*	*12*	*2.4*	*depth*	*open sea*			

This cluster brings themes of Titanic fight, the forces D needed to reach for from the deepest depths in order to fight for her life, drinking to the bottom. The central theme of marriage is followed with guilt and mistake – in the sense of looking over the unsuccessful trials and also missing the one that meant so much for her? A new theme is the fear-stupidity-flying, especially flying as the introduction of the new 'element' – air. This prompted me to think about the *puer* qualities of D's Animus – her non-stopping, sparkly, flighty mind and constant activities and also a heavy contrast when she touches the ground, triggered by some sad or disappointing event (Fly-fear and Death – inevitability might resonate with these remarks as well).

41	hurt	23	4.6	to be selfish	to be stupid		T	4
42	flower	35	7	that hippie sign	+		T	2
43	evil	22	4.3	anger	man – as human being		T	4
44	party	31	6.1	boredom	+		T	1
45	*fly*	*12*	*2.4*	*fear*	*+*			
46	*death*	*17*	*3.3*	*inevitability*	*+*			

Responses to SWs Hurt and Flower seem to me to be resulting in four CIs condensed following SW Evil, where the word 'anger' is uttered for the first time. If D is of a depressive structure, than I consider this especially significant. Given the way she describes the 'flowers' in the Context, it is something most natural, precious, wondrous and fragile to hurt. Perhaps her own inner soft and subtle nature. Maybe in her reactions to Evil one can hear the core of her deepest distrust in the world around her and see anger both as a potential and inhibitor of connection. I wonder whether her PT reaction to 'Party' was an echo of 'Evil'...

47	clean	23	4.6	false	problem		T	2
48	try	17	3.4	know	to be brave			3
49	sin	21	4.1	experience	+		T	2
50	home	18	3.5	tweed	+	tone of voice		1

This last cluster, as if in Shakespeare dramas, brings an epilogue. Continuing where the prologue started: Play – alley. When D was 14 her father bought her a green aba to make a coat. She still keeps it. D had a dream after we had finished the Context:

I see a big green squarish surface. Like tweed texture. In the central lower part my father collects small stones. They are all white with one that is black.

Context interview

Stimulus word: Free

Free space. No barriers, constraints, simply peace within, peaceful, blue, infinite, big, not without rules, but without norms. Simply that it is peace and endlessly big and that you draw happiness and energy from it. A house on the island H. comes to mind where we used to go all the time. When I look – I see a lighthouse to the right and a huge space behind. I always wondered what was there . . . I feel peace when I see that broadness. We used to go there between 7 and 22 years of age both summer and winter. I don't think I am very free. First I do not have a freedom to do all the time what I want. Before I usually did what I thought I had or should do. It is better now but I was rarely me. Freedom is when you are who you are and somebody either loves you or not. To be who you are is freedom for me.

Examination

I see the potential semantics of these references in three levels as D expressed them:

collective level: Inner position and state-of-being where one can be open to experience life and develop; it is also elemental – 'open sea' which could indicate the connection to the unconscious and access to it. It is important to mark that the way these references are given does not indicate unruly chaotic expanding energy, but rather the one that provides peace within natural rules. I am inclined to understand this level as Ego – Self relation, archetypal container for the growth of her authentic personality.

ancestral-developmental level (also a bridge between the collective and individual meaning): The experiences D had there between 7–22 years of age are potentially serving as a 'lighthouse' function of her psyche; they seem carry also positive experiences of her childhood drawing the allying forces supporting D's ability for insight. The light house is an important point of topographical relevance for D's psyche: It is not the private house on the island, it is on the ground (not the water), it sheds the light on darkness helping ships sailing on the water to orient and be safe. It seems that when in the 'lighthouse position', D can see what is going on, safe from the potentially overwhelming contents in the private house, but connected to it, having a firm ground underneath from the place she observes/experiences life, and at the same time very closely connected to the unconscious supporting the navigation of the content that comes from there by the light of insight. It would be interesting to explore the qualities of experiences and inheritance that D got there in her life (internalised imagoes) and how her parental and ancestral images live in her supporting her journey.

Reflecting upon D's last comments:

I don't think I am very free. First I do not have a freedom to do all the time what I want. Before I usually did what I thought I had or should do. It is better now but I was rarely me. Freedom is when you are who you are and somebody either loves you or not. To be who you are is freedom for me.

I wonder, given her dreams and reactions, whether she can be free only when she herself becomes aware of who she is – for this period of her wounded self and accepting it?

Stimulus word: Kiss

I constantly have that sound 'sljap'. I hated when my aunts and alike 'lick' me and hug me . . . oh how cute she is, oh how sweet and then they would pinch my cheek . . . uh it annoyed me enormously! I got fewest kisses from my father, everybody else was 'licking' me and I hated it. As a child I did not like to speak and they made me speak all the time. There was a teacher in my school who constantly forced me to speak (I was 4 years old). Even today I am quiet in a company of people I do not know well. I remember that she was pulling my hear so much, I still wouldn't speak, at the end when she stopped I told her 'You ass!' and then she started hugging me and kissing me so that I felt sick. Once I got beaten by my father when I was 8–9 years old with his belt and an hour after he came to me crying and apologising, he thought I ran away from home and there was a mad client who was threatening him . . . he got afraid that something happened to me. When he approached to me to kiss me I hated it and I still hear that 'sljap' sound . . . (she was quiet for a while, as if thinking of something else). . . It has nothing to do with romantic male-female kisses; I like those kinds of kisses.

Examination

Responses to the word 'kiss' seem to bring negative feelings mainly related to dishonesty, pretence and being hurt (aggression) behind that pretence. In all the examples D gave regarding to kisses are people that overtly or covertly hurt her, emotionally and physically. One does hear longing in D's offhand comment *I got fewest kisses from my father, everybody else were licking me* – as if she was expecting from her father (role?) not to execute such behavior. What these responses bring to mind is passive and open aggression, of which she was a victim during her entire childhood and also later in her life in a repetitive pattern. At the same time it seems that kiss is a token of true connection for D. We find again the element of water. As an archetypal image, kiss could be understood as a symbol of connection, exchange of soul, union.

Stimulus word: Naked

No constraints, it associates me of that freedom, nothing is constraining me. I never wanted to be naked, I remember being 3 years old and people looking at me . . . I remember my mother entering the kitchen in her night gown and my father shouting at her to 'cover herself' and that she should be ashamed to show herself like that in front of me (7–8 years of age). On my birthday my mother took me to the photographer to take a picture of me. She dressed me in the clothes I disliked and when I was 14 years of age I said I did not want to do it anymore. It was like doing a sentence, I cried every time. It was important to my mother that I looked as a doll. The only thing I liked was my knitted socks. They always went to people (and took me with them) without children. She liked combing my hair and making different coiffures. I was frustrated I couldn't be me. My only freedom was when I was with an animal and did whatever I wanted with it. My mother never bought anything new for me, I did not have my own coat till I was 16, I was inheriting other people's clothes. Nowadays I buy clothes uncontrollably and never have any. First thing she bought for me was a tweed jacket when I was 15. It was important to my father that I was dressed like a proper girl. My parents were never naked in front of me. I remember my potty. I had problems defecating (3–4 years of age). They made me sit on the potty for hours. Till 3 years ago, I was not able to empty my bowels regularly.

Examination

The theme of being herself continues here as well, shedding an additional light to Anima – Persona relation. In respect to the relationship with her mother, there is a pattern of trying to please the external demands to be accepted on one side, and at the same time not mirroring her genuine personality. In addition to her feeling inadequate, in D's thinking there is something wrong with her one can think of negative Animus who is misleading in nature. Inhibitions of expressing herself seem to be incorporated through the physiological dimension as well, with an important change 3 years ago. One pivotal connection to the true nature that D never seized to have was with animals. They are closest beings to her in life even now and her closest family, perhaps signaling still, on the symbolic level, her deepest need for resonating with nature (and her natural self), connection to her instincts and wild self. D's dogs have been winners of many trophies, always among first in dogs' exhibitions . . . One might think of 'dolls' and 'finger-direction' reaction . . . (SW 14), as well as re-enacting D's own experiences of being dressed up by her mother and photographed.

Stimulus word: Boss

I hate rules (norms), especially if I do not understand them. I did not like them as a child; I do not like them now. I hate when somebody tells me 'you have to'. It took me many years to understand that I don't have to; it is I want or do not want to, not I have to. I always had rules imposed on me (you must not sit at the table with grown up, you have to go to the shops, you have to be quiet, you must not talk back . . ., while you are under my roof it has to be like I want . . .). Where there are too many rules imposed – anarchy is created. In my work I always tried to develop and go up the ladder very quickly, to be one step above from others, so that those imposed rules are lesser, so that I could be more creative, make a decision not only obey.

Examination

The toll of too strict Animus, apparently in both of her parents (and aunts and uncles from both sides) and negative feminine, lack of setting the boundaries that constipated her expression and natural flow of life energy could be seen in D's challenges with superiors and significant others. The reaction she will get towards them is 'anarchy'. She would find herself in a position of a rebellion against the rules, she would feel the rules limiting and suffocating expression and often highly unjust. It is also interesting that D would have people 'above' her who would be very different to her and probably of the opposite type. There is a curious development of the 'qualities' in her 'bosses' through her career – from really abusive ones to a person she works for at the moment (seems to be dominant thinking type) whom she disagrees but respects highly and is able to disagree with high presence of emotional charge but at the same time with the more objective perspective and empathy.

Stimulus word: Family

It was always like in a beehive. Always too many people, my mother was 'tied' to her sister and I am absolutely positive that she loved them more than me. Aunt and uncle were teachers, extremely stern and my mother always went to them to solve their problems (for example their children ran away from home). It was always them (my cousins) who were better, harder working, created more in their lives (in fact – they are now miserable, they actually have nothing) I always had to be like them. I always hated them, even nowadays I do not have any contact with them. On the other side – my father had a brother with two children, nobles, good pupils, sportsmen . . . I had to be like them as well. I do not have a contact with them either. VOICE – noise: Gossiping, and then my mother and father would quarrel – from my father side very 'fine' and well educated, opposite from my mother side . . . always many voices, that were not ours. If it wasn't for my mother's huge bond with her sister . . . maybe my mother and father would stay longer together. My mother and father never had a common bedroom. I was once making spots with a stick on a freshly painted wall, my mother bit me so badly. She has never apologised to me. And so many times she was not right.

Examination

Here we got some stronger light on to the familial unconscious setup, forces traveling transgenerationally, charged with such a high potential – embodied in D's mother suicide. D said that her mother could not stand the pain any longer and decided to stop it. Her mother stopped. (It is perhaps worthwhile noticing that it was D's left breast that was diagnosed with cancer). It is interesting that D is working with 40–200 children who are creating music through improvisation and she always comments with a smile that it is very noisy and 'busy'. D speaks about a beehive, many different voices, noise and high frequency, high fluctuation of different energies. In her childhood it resulted with dissonant energy (parents would quarrel); in her present life the children make a high quality musical out of lot of 'noise'. I also think of a symbol of beehive for quite a few ancient civilisations when they reached their peak of prosperity and harmony, as a potential of development. I am also thinking about the dissonance between two different qualities that should be in a harmonious marriage: Village, 'ordinary', more simple people (D's mother family) and educated, 'sophisticated', urban (father's family) and how this disharmony was internalised in D's psyche. Enkidu and Gilgamesh. 'Natural' ('archaic') and 'civilised' man.

Reflecting upon D's words given here, perhaps it is that the developing of the raw material was interrupted so it remained in storming phase (Tuckman 1965) creating a neurotic circle. On the other side none of the families supported D's love for animals so through D's strongest devotion to animal care the gradient for this familial oppressed energy came into being.

D's last comment, apparently disconnected to the previous context, provoke an image of deliberate 'spoiling' the perfection in Islamic architecture – nothing in nature is one-sided. Furthermore, as if D wanted to add some content to the fresh beginning, continuing the process of the renovation of her parents' intimacy . . .

Stimulus word: Sick

I thought of not telling you but I will tell you. I got diagnosed with the breast cancer. I was in my home country at that time. When I went to oncology institute I wanted to die when I saw the cancer patients there. For quite a long while I did not want to do anything regarding the illness, just to let it go in its own course. Then I decided to go to my other country. I stayed at my friend and his wife after the surgery and was on chemo therapy. It was tough but I made it. I was alone and nobody except but my two best friends knew. I did not mind dying, just the pain. I had to be brave. Everything will pass . . . I have to go on. If I stop I will get ill. The only thing that matters is that nobody looks at me.

Examination

D's words bring back the dream with her V friend and the scars, especially the blackness of one scar in particular and her wonder of her friend not being connected to it. D's comments also remind me of the beach scene and nakedness – when she did not want to be naked, feeling shy (shame?) because something was wrong with her ... Now she actually misses a part of her body and people can actually see it. Apart from her very closest friends, nobody knows that she was ill at all. The key themes here could be pain, loneliness (existential loneliness and feeling isolated) – absence of support, need to move, and hope for the good outcome. I am thinking of the negative mother complex but also of a positive father complex (in the sense that things will turn out well). D's father seemed to be harsh, violent, highly critical but also he was the one who 'could' in the family. He was enterprising and was able to execute things perhaps in opposition to her mother who eventually stopped. I am also thinking about D's connection to animals – the connection to the innate knowledge of nature per excellence (healing power for ex.), therefore there could be a presence of a positive mother complex as well.

Stimulus word: Pray

To pray for what. For health. Every time I was supposed to pray and light the candles I did, but ... I am the one who can decide whether I will be ok or not. I do not understand people who find a church when they are not well. If I do not have peace with myself no church will help me. I do believe (not in priests), I am not a non-believer. I do not brag that I am a believer it is disgusting to me – bljak (like sljap). I do not believe that any of them is a true believer, it is all – mimicry.

BRAVE? – Me ...

Examination

I read here an awareness and maturity of a person who learned from life experience that there is a lot to be done with one's 'destiny' if one is aware and works on one's own world ('god within') discovering powers that are there. It feels it is with a pinch of sorrow (bitterness?) because D had to learn it due to absence of support – she was left to her own devices early in her life. In this respect I am also thinking of a sense of anger and longing in her reaction towards people who do find sense and help in going to church when they are not well – as if she is bothered by their ability to find comfort in the forces outside. Developmentally, it is the silence and dissonance as a result of the attempts of early childhood tuning. Negative mother and critical (abusive) father. But she is a believer. Again, there is a deeper force, connection to her natural religiosity, behind the negative experiences giving her support and hope.

Stimulus word: Marry

Nothing comes, but absolutely nothing. Point blank. I do not have a person, nor situation related to this. I do have a problem, guaranteed. Why when you marry, why do people always have incredible urge that now something needs to change. We are married now, now something needs to change. I fall in love with somebody with all the faults ... I wanted to change, but not somebody else changing me. I did change by my own will for somebody before ... what came to me then! I would consciously stop myself wanting to change somebody, to adjust. My friend has a habit to chew a toot-pick. My female friend, his partner keeps telling him – take the toot-pick out, stop eating that much ... grumping, grumping or being angry and silent ... that is marriage. A cage – because of this grumping. Returning the images of my mother and father and also some of my relationships. Why do I care ... why one has to get married in order to be socially successful?! Are you married? – they ask me, and if I am not, it must be something wrong with me ...

Examination

D herself makes a connection between her feeling towards marriage and her experiences of her parents' marriage. Here is again the theme of being herself and not somebody else in relation to the expectation of the other. D is also aware of her own need to change others and the positive willingness to change/adjust herself in a relationship when it is her conscious decision. The resistance to be who she is not because of the expectation of others is striking perhaps reflecting the huge suffering and pain she went through. The defense against that pain embodied in a token of a relationship as such – the marriage is obvious. It is also obvious D's wish to be in a relationship where she would be accepted for who she is. I wonder whether the amount of pain and the need to protect herself against it inhibited her to fight for the relationship she enjoyed so much? Or/and was it her (unconscious) feeling of something actually 'wrong' with her that made her give up on something that fulfilled her so much? She cannot be good enough for him, nor for the happiness she experiences, it cannot last, so it is better to end it now . . .? Since she had to be brave and not stop (meet her pain, have pity), could it be that 'what is wrong with her' now is the wounded D appearing on the stage (dream)? Can she 'marry' her, love her and support her for what she is? The internalised dynamics of the parental imagos seem to contaminate the archetypal image of marriage (union of opposites).

Stimulus word: Party

I simply cannot recall a party or wedding that I had a good time. Weddings – kitch parades. Parties – it comes down to talking to people I came with, drinking bear and smoking dope. And if among those 50 people there is somebody 'smart' and starts talking . . ., I immediately get quiet. I like to go out, I like to get together over dinner and talk with my friends, but not with 50 people . . . I do love my birthday, I make it the way I like, gather people I like . . . At the parties everybody speaks at the same time, I can't properly hear anybody . . . I did not like the disco clubs either. Smaller circle of friends I like,

I feel safe, people who will not mind if I spill something on me, drink a bit more . . . I love demonstrations. Anarchy. I love concerts. I would marry The Englishman tomorrow, because he was genuine. With him I have never felt him wanting to change me, or laugh at me if I say something silly. We could speak about everything. We laughed a lot, I always loved to go out with him. He did not like 50 people parties either. I did not have to make myself beautiful in order for him to like me. Happiness. Then I would define marriage as freedom and big space. If only I could have that feeling again – to be able to be quiet in peace, to be myself . . .

Examination

Exposure to the external life, participation in it, vulnerability. Here I find the circle of meaning rounding off with the return, or re-ligare to the collective level: Open see, peace, happy. To be herself. She is describing party of non-listening/hearing each other, noise, which reminds me of the beehive, voices and responses to 'family'. The way D reflects on this SW, especially in the semantic sequence, potentially reflects a formula of having positive experience of life: Having different voices expressed, listened to and heard properly brings marriage and a potential party – joie de vivre.

Stimulus word: Hurt

That somebody who is going to hurt you must be stupid. I do not understand how they have time to do these things – to hurt somebody. My father and my mother . . . such insults and bad words... What do I gain if I tell you – 'you are so ugly'... And then they would put me in the middle and ask me who was right. I will tell you directly what I think or I will keep quiet. I think it is a total stupidity either if I allow somebody to hurt me – somebody who will say to me something like how could you allow yourself to be so fat... My father used to tell me all the time how stupid I was. One of my partners used to tell me that I was stupid and brought me to the point when I actually thought either that I was ignorant or really stupid. It was only when I met The Englishman... My partner apologised later, I understood that he was not feeling ok in general that it was not me. It is selfish that I feel better if I hurt you. It is not clear to me and I do not want it to be clear to me. And who am I to judge... I do not like when people insult somebody. I feel sadness and if it is really a bad insult I get angry and then I want justice to be done.

Examination

D's words above seem very rational, ethical and proper. 'Too' rational. I am thinking that maybe this could be a defense against actually expressing her anger and a potential depressive structure. *I do not like when people insult somebody. I feel sadness and if it is really a bad insult I get angry and then I want justice to be done.* D's reaction to aggression towards her is sadness (result of her expression of anger was severely censored when she was a child). It has to be really a bad 'hurt' in order that she demands justice. I am thinking of D setting boundaries in her life and also about her illnesses. D is spending majority of her time caring about children that are hurt, trying to get justice for them. The reaction 'stupid' sheds additional light how powerful (and somehow 'final', non-discussible) that word is in her experience, terminating any attempt for anger to come out. I wonder that at some point the power of it helped not to stop... Perhaps it is the time now for her carefully to open for compassion for her own suffering and not feel stupid. I also note the mediating child and wiring into parental wounds.

Stimulus word: Flower

Oh yes! Flowers associated me with the smile and then to the hippy sign. Everything related to flowers calms me down, I love to work with flowers. I love to have flowers, it is beautiful and gentle. Poppy seed flower, ever so gentle creature, the petals, you need to take care of them and then it rewards you with something so beautiful. I could not pick a poppy-seed flower, ever. There is a fairy tale related with a poppy seed flower... It closes in the morning and opens in the evening, there are 3 petals, does not last long, few days, flower of May, sometimes September... Maiden's veil. Burnt by the sun, I took it back in to the shade. I grow flowers, the one called 'contempt' in my language is my favorite plant. I never know what kind of flower will come up, plus you don't need to water it. It is so tender, you think it will die, but it is actually so endurable... flowers from lilac to white, entire spectrum.

Examination

Who is D? How she grows and flourishes? As if this was 'a big dream' that we usually do not analyse, rather just allowing scents of psyche to enrich our life in entire spectrum... D could not remember the exact fairytale. I am thinking about Vasilisa The Wise and the poppy seed as a food of dead – lowering down the control of consciousness, ability to be and relax...?

Interpretation hypothesis

Map of complexes

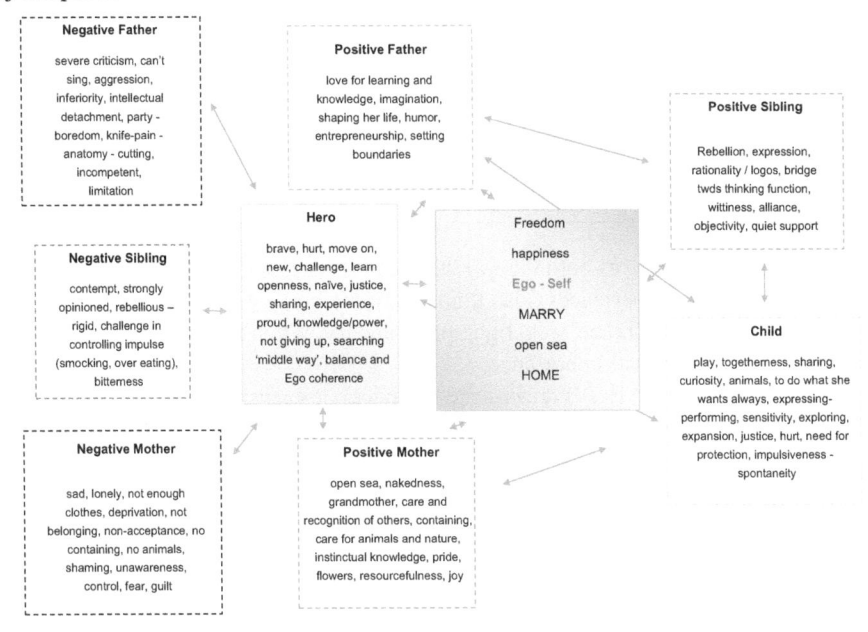

Negative Father
severe criticism, can't sing, aggression, inferiority, intellectual detachment, party - boredom, knife-pain - anatomy - cutting, incompetent, limitation

Positive Father
love for learning and knowledge, imagination, shaping her life, humor, entrepreneurship, setting boundaries

Positive Sibling
Rebellion, expression, rationality / logos, bridge twds thinking function, wittiness, alliance, objectivity, quiet support

Hero
brave, hurt, move on, new, challenge, learn openness, naïve, justice, sharing, experience, proud, knowledge/power, not giving up, searching 'middle way', balance and Ego coherence

Freedom
happiness
Ego - Self
MARRY
open sea
HOME

Negative Sibling
contempt, strongly opinioned, rebellious – rigid, challenge in controlling impulse (smocking, over eating), bitterness

Child
play, togetherness, sharing, curiosity, animals, to do what she wants always, expressing-performing, sensitivity, exploring, expansion, justice, hurt, need for protection, impulsiveness - spontaneity

Negative Mother
sad, lonely, not enough clothes, deprivation, not belonging, non-acceptance, no containing, no animals, shaming, unawareness, control, fear, guilt

Positive Mother
open sea, nakedness, grandmother, care and recognition of others, containing, care for animals and nature, instinctual knowledge, pride, flowers, resourcefulness, joy

'Noughts and crosses' – a few notes for discussion

The complexes shown are a limited selection for discussion. Relevant affects will be elaborated in the Summary. My initial hypothesis is that the Child complex has the strongest concentration of libido. I am considering D as a constellation type in regards to the process of the WAE. Given D's very challenging life, from her very early days, violence, illness, war, mother's suicide, her current acceptance that she will probably not have children of her own, I consider the appearance of the wounded character in her dream of greatest importance. Thinking of D's dreams and recent development I am inclined to think that D is ready (and has already started) to get to know this character better and carefully and to gradually integrate it as part of herself. It is in that character where we find, perhaps, the deepest dynamic generating the flow of energies (some of which are discussed in this book) constellating different complexes: It is presented by D's unconscious in the game of X-Ox.

I here explain my understanding of the 'X' as cross or 'four' = man as *mana* in a circle (horizon or Earth) resulting with the symbol $\otimes$ from Jung's amplification (CW 7 paras. 374–406), as a token of D's soul 'United Kingdom'.

Synopsis of the main findings

Several points came out as key regarding both the understanding and future work:
Reassembling the experience in order to transform them (also having in mind the dream with a friend with the wounds), emotions needed to connect to the experiences and the connecting principle – new with old.

experience	new sin old	*reassembling*
free	free naked learn happy	*connecting new with old*
stupid	weak hurt fear pity	*emotions needed to connect to the experiences*

If we consider the word *brave* as both the *spiritus movens* for D and the gate where she is opening for the re-connecting experiences (also thinking of the brave child's 'contempt', or *in spite of*...), then we extrapolate: Choice, sick, fight, pride and try. When D is brave, D is on the move. And, as D says, it is of survival importance.

Given the data from the WAE, D's dreams and behaviour, it seems indeed that the Ego is at great extent identified with *moving*. There is a charged libido in this brave child and the source of life power.

Bravery in speaking out things that are the underlying opposite to the mainstream, being highly spirited, but sad behind the spiritedness leads to the image of the fool. The fool is closely connected to the king, speaks out what nobody dares and is sad behind the mask (the clown). The Fool brings the 'crazy wisdom', a different perspective and seems to work opposite to the Persona archetype (but could itself become a persona).

It is interesting that the fool is presented in the major arcane (Golden Down, Deck of Toth) with animals and a child and has a mark 'O' (X-O?), opens and closes the arcana. It also teaches through play (jester). When thinking about the king's fool I wonder about the actual dependent relation to 'the king' (for example D's own treatment of her dog, her utmost effort to meet the expectations of her employer, and the like).

Constantly on the move, the brave, resilient child, the fool . . . how does it relate to D's wounded body? The mother complex is deeply connected to the body, and the connection could be seen in the absence of support and proper nourishment, D not being connected to her body and perhaps self-punishment and deep shame in relation to the body. The illness D went through, her disregard of her health, eating habits, intensive smoking, no exercise and healthy routines bring the awareness of woundedness, fragility, danger and also D's capacity of moving, rebelling and taking all the missions her Ego is so closely related with. It raises the questions of boundaries. Furthermore, it raises the question of anger; profound anger due to abandonment, injustice, neglect, not being seen and nurtured, deprivation of love, support and care, and the termination of life of her unborn child. Hence also the notion being 'on the move' between anger, sadness, loneliness, emptiness and 'drama', intensive experiences, moving in a see-saw manner searching for the middle way, more healthy balance.

At the WAE examination discussion, the issue of D being triangulated in relation to her mother and father and also between the two wider families constantly throughout her childhood was emphasised and brought to light a potential question of borderline features (see Appendix). This insight is precious in understanding the dynamic and also the origin of D's space and 'freedom', the crucial issue of being herself, thus also giving permission to be loved.

It seems that D is experiencing life mostly from 'Child' perspective, which implies her identification with the (transgenerational) trauma. Based on the WAE findings and D's dreams during the WAE process, it seems that D is ready to connect more to her (wounded) self and thus start differentiating from the trauma and start discovering her deeper, more mature self.

Indications for the therapeutic work

It seems that the Jungian world of working with the unconscious is a mother tongue of both the brave child and the fool, so there is a great libido motivation related to D's commitment to pursue her analysis. I would say that even deeper is the call of the Great Mother for D to find her way home, by the open sea.

D expressed a myriad of living symbols which are a precious source for our potential work together. Images she produced in the Context interview could be material for creating stories, paintings and sound/music. Her experiences and references to her body could be another guide and area of exploration (Jungian body work). Perhaps the bottom line is that our work together should be a safe space for D to explore, express and discover her deep identity, the very process that might hold and facilitate the healing of the split. When she is ready, she might look at or connect with the blackness of the scars and discover the colours.

It is important for there to be time and space where D could perhaps be free.

The WAE experience helped to inform my potential roles in our future work, such as:

- holding the volatile dynamics of the opposites rather than going into problem-solving (the depth and the extreme volume of the opposites, and the intensity of D's experience of the tension of opposites in particular made me more sentitised and moved)
- being curious about her own thoughts and methods rather than giving her answers especially when she comes with direct demand for advice or answer (empowerment)
- patience, faith in Nature and sensitivity to gentleness and innate power of flowers in her own psyche

Furthermore, our work should be a holding space for her finding her 'middle way', a firm container for expressing her affective states and, in time, hopefully, transforming into more balanced and mature coping mechanisms (reducing impulsivity and especially acting them out). Establishing mutual trust in our relationship might facilitate D building more sustainable human relationships in her life.

Reflections on the AE experience for the candidate's individuation process

The experience of both conducting and analyzing the data of the WAE brought to awareness several topics which I find resonating with my own individuation process:

- Negative mother
- 'Child' – especially as regards 'rebellion' and strong connection to animals and flowers
- Spiritedness – especially hiding behind wittiness and humor

This awareness made me particularly alert to my own projections and cautioned me about my potential interpretation biases.

I was reflecting on why this experience in the form of WAE took place now in my life, and it provided additional light onto how much these two complexes determined my roles in life and coloured my life experiences and reading of reality. I can see now myself not identified with these roles and being able to recognise my automatic reactions and being able not to act them out but to take them into consideration, feeling empathy to the wounded characters of my psyche. I am reminded of Jung's view on our deep connections with our clients, and I remain grateful for the learning this client brought to my life.

Appendix: Borderline personality disorder short description and symptoms

'People with borderline personality disorder have a strong fear of abandonment or being left alone. Even though they want to have loving and lasting relationships, the fear of being abandoned often leads to mood swings and anger. It also leads to impulsiveness and self-injury that may push others away' (Mayo Clinic 2024). Note: The image of self-injury was strongly presented in D's dream.

Borderline personality disorder usually begins by early adulthood. The condition is most serious in young adulthood. Mood swings, anger and impulsiveness often get better with age. But the main issues of self-image and fear of being abandoned, as well as relationship issues, go on (Mayo Clinic 2024).

Symptoms may include (Mayo Clinic 2024):

- A strong **fear of abandonment**. This includes going to extreme measures so you're not separated or rejected, even if these fears are made up.
- **A pattern of unstable, intense relationships**, such as believing someone is perfect one moment and then suddenly believing the person doesn't care enough or is cruel.
- **Quick changes in how you see yourself**. This includes shifting goals and values, as well as seeing yourself as bad or as if you don't exist.
- Periods of stress-related paranoia and loss of contact with reality. These periods can last from a few minutes to a few hours.
- **Impulsive and risky behavior**, such as gambling, dangerous driving, unsafe sex, spending sprees, binge eating, drug misuse, or sabotaging success by suddenly quitting a good job or ending a positive relationship.
- Threats of suicide or self-injury, often in response to fears of separation or rejection.
- **Wide mood swings** that last from a few hours to a few days. These mood swings can include periods of being very happy, irritable or anxious or feeling shame.
- Ongoing **feelings of emptiness**.
- Inappropriate, **strong anger**, such as losing your temper often, being sarcastic or bitter, or physically fighting.

Notes

1 Please see the initial reflection on the word 'free' in the Response reactions chapter.
2 When D told me about her mother's suicide, she kindly asked me not to mention it at all because she is not ready to 'go there'.

References

Jung, CG 1953/1977, *Two Essays on Analytical Psychology*, CW 7.
Jung, CG 2000, *The Collected Works of C. G. Jung* (CW), eds. H Read, M Fordham, G Adler and W McGuire, trans. RFC Hull, Princeton University Press, Princeton.
Kast, V 1980, *Excerpts in English from 'Das assoziationsexperiment in der therapeutischen praxis'*, trans. Irene Gad, Bonz Verlag, Fellback-Oeffingen.
Lepori, D 2015, 'Introduction to WAE', [Seminar notes], C G Jung Institute, Zurich.
Mayo Clinic. 2024, 'Borderline personality disorder'. Visited March 6. <www.mayoclinic.org/diseases-conditions/borderline-personality-disorder/symptoms-causes/syc-20370237>.
Tuckman, B 1965, 'Developmental sequence in small groups', *Psychological Bulletin*, vol. 63, no. 6, pp. 384–399. <doi: 10.1037/h0022100>.

11 The Word Association Experiment and the DSM/ICD categories

John O'Brien

Overview of ICD and DSM

The International Classification of Diseases (ICD) and *Diagnostic and Statistical Manual of Mental Disorders* (DSM) classification systems are systems for mental disorders and diseases. They both provide manualised codes which are used to provide statistics to health authorities and related organisations dealing with resource allocation. There are similarities and differences in between both systems which are supported by the various editions of their handbooks. Both classify health conditions, and the DSM focuses only on mental disorders.

The ICD has traditionally focused on observable and objective manifestations of ill health, whereas the early versions of the DSM were strongly influenced by the US psychoanalytic movement. The trend has been towards a unification of the systems in the interest of improved patient care.

The early US psychoanalytic orientation in the DSM was criticised as being encapsulated, i.e. founded upon theories of the unconscious which were not refutable. It seems likely that this was partly a result of the growth of the 'psycho-analytic industry', which relied increasingly on theoretical models abstracted from infant observation and which was preoccupied with the advancement and defense of different theoretical schools within its own body of knowledge. Since the inception of the DSM III and through to the DSM V, the orientation has shifted towards the categorisation of diagnoses based on present signs and symptoms (see Glossary).

Further background to the ICD

The ICD originated in the late 19th century and, since that time, has become the world's main reference for the classification of diseases. It provides statistical data on the causes and consequences of disease and death over a wide range of countries and of countries over time. Although the latest version, the ICD 11, has been in effect since January 1922, adoption has been slow, with practitioners frequently using the ICD 10 as a reference point. It had been approved by the 72nd World Assembly in 2019.

According to Raminani (2024) the first international classification of diseases was adopted in 1893 by the International Statistical Institute. It was based on the work of Bertillon (1880), a French quantitative social scientist. Interestingly, his 1893 presentation took place in the US, at the Chicago Conference of the International Statistical Institute, and four years later, in 1897, his system of classification was adopted by the American Health Association. The following year, it was recommended for use in the US, Canada and Mexico. In 1948, the World Health Organization (WHO) assumed responsibility for the ICD.

DOI: 10.4324/9781032716572-11

The ICD became increasingly detailed through repeated revision, particularly after 1948, when the World Health Organization (WHO) assumed responsibility for publishing the ICD and began collecting international data for all general epidemiological surveillance and health management purposes. WHO significantly revised the ICD in the 1980s and early 1990s. The resulting three-volume work, known as ICD-10 (International Statistical Classification of Diseases and Related Health Problems), was published in 1992; it eventually replaced the two-volume ICD-9 in countries worldwide that used the classification. The ICD became a core classification of the WHO Family of International Classifications (WHO-FIC).

There are eleven publications of the ICD, and a significant landmark was the publication of the ICD 10, with the most recent having been adopted by the World Health Assembly in 2019 and implemented in 2022.

The ICD 11

As of 2024, WHO describes its contemporary purpose, uses and highlights as follows:

ICD serves a broad range of uses globally and provides critical knowledge on the extent, causes and consequences of human disease and death worldwide via data that is reported and coded with the ICD. Clinical terms coded with ICD are the main basis for health recording and statistics on disease in primary, secondary and tertiary care, as well as on cause of death certificates. These data and statistics support payment systems, service planning, administration of quality and safety, and health services research. Diagnostic guidance linked to categories of ICD also standardises data collection and enables large scale research.

ICD purpose and uses

As a classification and terminology, ICD-11 (WHO 2019):

- allows the systematic recording, analysis, interpretation and comparison of mortality and morbidity data collected in different countries or regions and at different times;
- ensures semantic interoperability and reusability of recorded data for the different use cases beyond mere health statistics, including decision support, resource allocation, reimbursement, guidelines and more.

ICD-11 highlights

- Legally mandated health data standard (WHO Constitution and Nomenclature Regulations)
- In effect from January 2022
- Conceptual framework independent of language and culture
- Integration of terminology and classification
- End-to-end digital solution (API, tools, online and offline)
- Up-to-date scientific knowledge
- Comparable statistics and semantic interoperability – for 150 years
- ICD-11 is accessible to everybody.
- ICD-11 is distributed under a Creative Commons Attribution-NoDerivs 3.0 IGO license.
- ICD-11 enables, for the first time, the counting of traditional medicine services and encounters.
- The 11th revision is more extensive and has greater implications for what can be done with the ICD, and how, than any revision since the 6th, in 1948.

In some respects the approach to DSM diagnosis appears to have shifted from traditional classification to a more holistic approach. This is perhaps most apparent in the case of personality disorders.

> In contrast to the established categorical approach to Personality Disorders (PDs) in ICD-10 and DSM-5 (i.e., 8–12 distinct types), the ICD-11 focuses on global and shared features that apply to *all* PDs . . . These features comprise a substantial part of the general diagnostic requirements for the presence of a PD. Accordingly, the practitioner or researcher must diagnose a *PD based on a global evaluation of self- and interpersonal functioning, cognitive, emotional, and behavioral manifestations, and psychosocial impairment and distress*.
> (Bach, Kramer et al. 2022; my italics)

A contextual explanation is provided in the WAE sub-chapter.

This development suggests an integration of psycho-social theory (as popularised in the use of the Global Assessment of Functioning scale in the DSM (DSM III (see Glossary and Appendix 3), and the paragraph as a whole might also apply as a description of the WAE. Of particular interest here is the notion of *negative affectivity*.

Bach et al. (2022) state that 'some evidence suggests that the trait domain of negative affectivity explains a large amount of personality pathology observed in mental health services'.

> Metaphorically, Negative Affectivity may be compared to the juice that serves as base ingredient in many different cocktails. However, while such 'cocktails' of trait domains may be clinically relevant, it remains questionable whether they actually capture the content of the familiar PD types that we usually treat.

The WAE, of course, is an instrument *par excellence* of identifying negative affect and, its developmental sources as well as its present manifestations and its likely trajectory.

Further background to the DSM

Since the publication of the DSM1 in 1952, the DSM has undergone three major stages of development, each reflecting different balances between medical classification and other schools of thought. Its forerunner was the *Statistical Manual for the Use of Institutions for the Insane* (The National Committee for Mental Hygiene, Bureau of Statistics 1918) and was biologically oriented, being in line with Kraeplin's approach (Brückner 2023).

The first stage, represented by the DSM1 and DSM2, was based on the psychodynamic approach which had gained acceptance in Britain and the United States as a result of the successful treatment of trauma victims of the World Wars. Psychiatry expanded from the exclusive use of organic biological models to include both psychoanalytic and environmental views and the recognition of a continuum of mental disorders reflecting milder stressors.

According to Kawa and Giordano (2012):

> the APA Committee on Nomenclature and Statistics sought to create a new classification system: The first edition of the *Diagnostic and Statistical Manual of Mental Disorders (DSM-I)*, which was officially released in 1952. This compendium included 102 broadly-construed diagnostic categories that were based upon psychodynamic etiological explanations, and were accordingly subdivided into two major groups of mental disorders: 1) conditions

assumedly caused by organic brain dysfunction (associated with somatic disturbances such as intoxication, trauma, or a variety of physiological diseases), and 2) conditions presumed to result from the effect(s) of socio-environmental stressors on individuals.

The second stage was represented by the DSM III (APA 1980) under the influence of Robert Spitzer. The emphasis on aetiology was replaced by focus on evidence patterns of signs and symptoms.

The third stage was the DSM IV (1994), DSM-IV-TR (2000) and DSM V (2013). Britannica (2024) states:

> Subsequent editions continued to expand the manual by incorporating current clinical research. The 1994 edition, DSM-IV, detailed nearly 300 disorders and was updated in a 'text revision' called the in 2000. DSM-5, unveiled in 2013, included the addition of newly recognized disorders, such as hoarding disorder and skin-picking disorder, as well as revisions to diagnostic criteria for existing conditions. The work was heavily criticized, however, for lowering the diagnostic threshold for mental disorders by adopting broader diagnostic criteria and for being based largely on subjective criteria rather than biological factors implicated in mental illness. A text revision of the DSM-5, called the DSM-5-TR, was published in 2022.

Summary of key features

Tyrer (2014) gives a simple summary of the key features of the ICD and DSM as follows:

ICD

- Official world classification
- Intended for use by all health practitioners
- Special attention given to primary care and low- and middle-income countries
- Major focus on clinical utility (planned for ICD-11) with reduction of number of diagnoses
- Provides diagnostic descriptions and guidance but does not employ operational criteria

DSM

- US classification (but used in many other countries)
- Used primarily by psychiatrists
- Focused mainly on secondary psychiatric care in high-income countries
- Tends to increase the number of diagnoses with each succeeding revision
- Diagnostic system depends on operational criteria using a polythetic system for most conditions (i.e. combination of criteria that need not all be the same)
- Use with transdiagnostic classification

WAE and links to DSM and ICD categories

It is generally accepted that psychotherapy is useful for particular categories of mental disorders. For example, Leichsenring and Klein's (2014, p. 1) review of the effectiveness of psychotherapy presents results from randomised controlled trials (RTCs) naming particular diagnostic categories of:

> common mental disorders, including depressive disorders, anxiety disorders, somatoform disorders, personality disorders, eating disorders, complicated grief, post traumatic stress disorder (PTSD), and substance-related disorders.

Also, in his 2013 report, Roesler, describing historical and current research into the efficacy and effectiveness of Jungian psychotherapy, advocates the use of the Word Association Test as an adjunct for the diagnosis and treatment for particular disorders and considers it worthy of further research (see Chapter 12).

The WAE provides complementary data which both is based on the past and present experiences of the patient and links complexes to sections of aetiology. Recent research has proven its evidence base (see Chapter 11), and the protocol includes observation of signs, elicitation of symptoms and identification of particular causal factors, such as childhood abuse. It also adds the important dimension of shared meaning of these factors.

Based on Wampold and Imel's (2015) research into therapeutic efficacy and effectiveness (see Chapter 12) and according to observations made in our research, practice and teaching, the explicit integration of common (largely humanistic) factors into the practice of delivering the WAE appears to enhance therapeutic benefit.

Insofar as the linkage of the outputs of the WAE points to the factors which are common to specific groups of mental disorders, then the WAE can be a useful adjunct to DSM and ICD users.

An example is provided in what follows.

Example

Here is a hypothetical example of a structure of a typical PTSD assessment which could be made by an analyst in accordance with the requirements of a particular governing organisation. It does not refer to any known patients but gives a composite picture of how the WAE can complement standard assessment approaches, in this case, the Clinician-administered PTSD scale for DSM 1V. The DSM 1V and DSM V classifications are given.

Assessment

Method used

The assessment was made as a natural element of the early stages of psychotherapy. It was completed on a particular date not specified here.

1a. The diagnostic is made in accordance with the guidance issued by the governing organisation using the Clinician-administered PTSD scale for DSM 1V.
1b. For the purposes of psycho-social planning, a multi-axial diagnostic assessment was made in accordance with the DSM1V guideline with differential diagnoses for Axis 1.
2. For other purposes a DSM 5 assessment is also given.

Transcripts of the sessions (lightly edited for understanding) are attached. (They are not actually included here, but are shared with the client as Rogerian summary and reflection and for the building of shared meaning).

1a) CLINICIAN-ADMINISTERED PTSD SCALE FOR DSM-IV.

309.81 Post-traumatic Stress Disorder, Chronic.

1b) MULTI-AXIAL DIAGNOSTIC ASSESSMENT

Axis 1 309.81 Post-traumatic Stress Disorder, Chronic.
        296.35 Major Depressive Disorder, Recurrent, Severe Without Psychotic Features, Without Inter-episode Recovery.
Axis 2 None
Axis 3 None
Axis 4 313.82 Identity Problem
        V61 Partner Relational Problem
        V62.89 Phase of Life Problem
        995.54 Physical Abuse of Child (Victim of Child Abuse)
        995.52 Neglect of Child (Victim of Child neglect)
Axis 5 GAS = 31 (on commencement of therapy)

2) DSM 5 ASSESSMENT
   309.81 (F43 10) Post Traumatic Stress Disorder, Without Dissociative Expression, Without Delayed Expression.
   296.35 (F33.2) Major Depressive Disorder, Recurrent, Severe Without Psychotic Features.

Association Experiment

The Association Experiment was conducted in accordance with the ethical guidelines of the administering clinic and the relevant Institute of the International Association of Analytical Psychology.

The findings from the anamnesis and the WAE protocol are as follows:

1 A pattern of childhood deprivation and abuse was identified by the patient.
2 The patient associated this with subsequent traumatic experiences.
3 The patient associated this with present life circumstances.
4 The patient's views were supported by reenactments evidenced during the course of the WAE and feedback.
5 These were consistent transference and counter-transference analysis.
6 Parental complexes were characterised by feelings of:

- Injury
- Disorientation
- Abandonment, separation and loss
- Physical abuse
- Fear/Powerlessness
- Rage

These were related to 'The Loss of Good Authority' complex.

The patient has resources related to her religious and cultural heritage.

She benefits from psychiatric management of distressing effects and uses access to medical help as needed.

Given the ego strength assessment, and working alliance built during the WAE, potential for separation from the complexes over a 90-session period of analytic therapy seems possible.

Here it can be seen how the WAE can pick up and manage common factor causes of mental stress and disorder, which can result in a coherent group of diagnoses. Approached solely through ICD/DSM classifications there are risks that:

a not all comorbidities are diagnosed
b signs and symptoms are observed recorded as 'present' or 'not present' can miss potential root or significant contributory causes and result in less healing or curative management

The example perhaps helps WAE practitioner to keep in mind that whatever the psychiatric diagnosis.

> Child maltreatment can lead to serious mental health concerns, including anxiety, depression, substance use disorders, eating disorders, dissociative identity disorder, and post-traumatic stress disorder (PTSD).
>
> (McLean Hospital 2024)

For the purposes of collaboration with other clinicians, it can be helpful for analysts to consider the relationship between findings from the WAE and common factors as contributing to the various diagnoses and categories thereof.

Use with transdiagnostic classification

It must also be said that the general philosophy and categorisations of the ICD and DSM can be called into question. For example, Dalgleish et al. (2020) provide a good critique of the ICD and DSM systems and offer a new 'transdiagnostic' approach to mental health problems:

> Without doubt, the diagnostic paradigm offers some clear benefits to clinical and research practice: It provides a *lingua franca* for describing clusters of symptoms that facilitates communication between users of services, clinicians and researchers; it sets out a common metric for research programs; and it provides an organizing principle for the development and evaluation of diagnosis-led assessment and treatment approaches. Finally, for some, the biomedical model at the heart of the diagnostic approach also brings legitimacy to the suffering that is experienced, reducing stigma and deflecting pejorative judgments that mental ill health reflects some form of personal weakness on the part of the diagnosed.
>
> Despite these advantages of the diagnostic paradigm, there is a gathering apprehension that the taxonomic approach instantiated in the DSM and ICD runs counter to the available clinical and research evidence and may hamper our understanding of mental ill health and consequently how we manage and treat mental distress.
>
> (Dalgleish et al. 2020)

The authors emphasise that despite the historical momentum and widespread influence of the diagnostic rubric, there is an emerging and growing consensus that such psychiatric nosologies may be reaching the limits of their research and clinical utility. In their place, there is gathering support for a 'transdiagnostic' approach that cuts across the traditional diagnostic boundaries or, more radically, sets them aside altogether to provide novel insights into how we might understand mental health difficulties. This transdiagnostic approach extends beyond issues of taxonomy. Removing the distinctions between proposed psychiatric taxa at the level of classification opens up new ways of conceptualising the underlying theories and processes implicated in mental ill health and provides a platform for novel ways of thinking about onset, maintenance, and clinical treatment and recovery from experiences of disabling mental distress.

The transdiagnostic model proposed by Dalgleish et al is radical in that it provides a new conceptual framework for diagnosis and treatment. This might be of interest to WAE practitioners who have similar objections to standard psychiatric approaches, as the WAE as an evidence-based instrument nutriment which takes into account deep perspectives of the patient is compatible with both. While a discussion of this topic is beyond the scope of this manual, our aim here aim is simply to note the trend of transdiagnostic diagnosis as in accordance with the identification of common aetioligies associated with discrete mental disorders within the existing classifications. Our note is offered in the spirit of greater collaborative working between analysts and psychiatrists in the interest of individual and collective patient health.

A specific transdiagnostic approach to commonalities of the structure of mental disorders was proposed by Slade and Watson (2006). The abstract is provided here:

> **Background:** Patterns of co-occurrence among the common mental disorders may provide information about underlying dimensions of psychopathology. The aim of the current study was to determine which of four models best fits the pattern of co-occurrence between 10 common DSM-IV and 11 common ICD-10 mental disorders.
> **Method:** Data were from the Australian National Survey of Mental Health and Well-Being (NSMHWB), a large-scale community epidemiological survey of mental disorders. Participants consisted of a random population-based sample of 10641 community volunteers, representing a response rate of 78%. DSM-IV and ICD-10 mental disorder diagnoses were obtained using the Composite International Diagnostic Interview (CIDI), version 2.0. Confirmatory factor analysis (CFA) was used to assess the relative fit of competing models.
> **Results:** A hierarchical three-factor variation of a two-factor model demonstrated the best fit to the correlations among the mental disorders. This model included a distress factor with high loadings on major depression, dysthymia, generalized anxiety disorder (GAD), post-traumatic stress disorder (PTSD) and neurasthenia (ICD-10 only); a fear factor with high loadings on social phobia, panic disorder, agoraphobia and obsessive-compulsive disorder (OCD); and an externalizing factor with high loadings on alcohol and drug dependence. The distress and fear factors were best conceptualized as subfactors of a higher order internalizing factor.
> **Conclusions:** A greater focus on underlying dimensions of distress, fear and externalization is warranted.

Such emotional states as well (as the whole range) are frequently identified in the WAE, together with their underlying psychological causes which are meaningful to the patient but which can escape recognition by all parties until they emerge (from the unconscious). The research supports not only a close look at emotional states (and behaviours) common to a range of disorders but also their aetiologies.

Summary

Complexes identified during the WAE have a developmental dimension which can be overlooked or underestimated in the ICD and DSM classifications. For example negative parental complexes can, in turn, produce positive or negative authority complexes. Practically speaking these can show up in recollections (cognitive and/or felt) of early childhood and adolescence deprivation and abuse. Such clusters of memories, to the extent that they have been traumatic, can result in (internalised and externalised) difficulties which appear autonomously. They are psycho-social in that they both are intra-psychic and behaviourally/socially present (see GAS scale, Appendix 3). They can, for example (in the case of PTSD), be root causes of intrusive thought and images as well as problematic relationships on the other. These factors might also contribute to classifiable conditions such as anxiety and depression and even to psychotic conditions.

The complexes identified in the WAE can therefore provide useful information which is not only useful as a *per se* in Jungian analysis but which can also inform standard psychiatric classification and treatment and is not incompatible with transdiagnostic models.

References

American Psychiatric Association (APA). 2022, *Diagnostic and Statistical Manual of Mental Disorders* (5th ed., text rev.). Visited March 11. <doi: 10.1176/appi.books.9780890425787>.
American Psychiatric Association (APA). 1952, DSM-I.
American Psychiatric Association (APA). 1968, DSM-II.
American Psychiatric Association (APA). 1980, DSM-III.
American Psychiatric Association (APA). 1994, DSM-IV.
American Psychiatric Association (APA). 2000, DSM-IV-TR.
American Psychiatric Association (APA). 2013, DSM V.
Bach, B, Kramer, U, Doering, S et al. 2022, *The ICD-11 Classification of Personality Disorders: A European Perspective on Challenges and Opportunities*. Visited March 11, 2024. <doi: 10.1186/s40479-022-00182-00>.
Bertillon, J 1880, *La statistique humaine de la france; naissance mariage mort*, Baillière, Paris.
Britannica. 2024, *Diagnostic and Statistical Manual of Mental Disorders*. Visited March 11, 2024. <www.britannica.com/topic/Diagnostic-and-Statistical-Manual-of-Mental-Disorders>.
Brückner, B 2023, 'Emil Kraepelin as a historian of psychiatry – one hundred years on', *History of Psychiatry*, vol. 34, no. 2, pp. 111–129. <doi: 10.1177/0957154X221143613>.
Dalgleish, T, Black, M, Johnston, D, Bevan, A 2020, 'Transdiagnostic approaches to mental health problems: Current status and future directions', *Journal of Consulting and Clinical Psychology*, vol. 88, no. 3, pp. 179–195. <doi: 10.1037/ccp0000482. PMID: 32068421; PMCID: PMC7027356.rueger RF>.
Kawa, S, Giordano, J 2012, 'A brief historicity of the diagnostic and statistical manual of mental disorders: Issues and implications for the future of psychiatric canon and practice', *Philosophy, Ethics and Humanities in Medicine*, vol. 7, no. 2. <doi: 10.1186/1747-5341-7-2. PMID: 22243976; PMCID: PMC3282636>.
Leichsenring, F, Klein, S 2014, 'Evidence for psychodynamic psychotherapy in specific mental disorders: A systematic review', *Psychoanalytic Psychotherapy*, vol. 28, no. 1, pp. 4–32. <doi: 10.1080/02668734.2013.865428>.
McLean Hospital. 2024, *Understanding Child Abuse*. Visited March 23. <https://www.mcleanhospital.org/essential/effects-child-abuse>.
The National Committee for Mental Hygiene, Bureau of Statistics 1918, 'Statistical manual for the use of institutions for the insane, *American Journal of Psychiatry*, vol. 75, no. 2, p. 301. <doi: 10.1176/ajp.75.2.301>.
Raminani, S 2024, 'International classification of diseases', *Encyclopedia Britannica*. Visited March 6, 2024. <www.britannica.com/topic/International-Classification-of-Diseases. Accessed 6 March 2024>.
Roesler, C 2013, 'Evidence for the effectiveness of Jungian psychotherapy: A review of empirical studies', *Behavioral Science*, vol. 24, no. 3, pp. 562–575. <doi: 10.3390/bs3040562. PMID: 25379256; PMCID: PMC4217606>.
Slade, T, Watson, D 2006, 'The structure of common DSM-IV and ICD-10 mental disorders in the Australian general population', *Psychological Medicine*, vol. 36, no. 11, pp. 1593–1600. <doi: 10.1017/S0033291706008452. Epub 2006 Aug 2. PMID: 16882356>.
Tyrer, P 2014, 'A comparison of DSM and ICD classifications of mental disorder', *Advances in Psychiatric Treatment*, vol. 20, no. 4, pp. 280–285. <doi: 10.1192/apt.bp.113.011296>.
Wampold, B, Imel, Z 2015, *The great psychotherapy debate: The evidence for what makes psychotherapy work*, Routledge, New York.
World Health Organization (WHO) 2019, *International statistical classification of diseases and related health problems* (11th ed.). Visited March 11 2024. <https://icd.who.int/>.

12 Research

John O'Brien

Introduction

To recap, Jung's Word Association Test began with a series of experiments designed with a view to producing tests for mental disorders, especially for (what is now termed) schizophrenia. Although these initial experiments were not successful, they led to the formulation of Jung's theory of complexes, which became the focus for a key strand of his research. However, having failed to produce a satisfactory test as originally conceived and following disagreements with Bleuler, Jung's research programme at the Burghölzi was declined in 1909, and he ceased his experimental studies to establish his own practice. This coincided with increased private focus on his 'most difficult experiment': His self-exploration recorded in the Black Books and the Red Book.

Nonetheless, his early experiments continued to make an impact, especially in the United States, where they resonated with the trend of devising instruments for the psychiatric diagnoses of specific mental disorders, for academic research and for clinical psychology (mainly personality assessments). Over the last 125 years, there have been significant further developments in the research and practice of the WAE/WAT, informed by developments in Jungian analysis and general psychotherapy. The version of the WAE training in this manual is a new articulation of Jung's work into which these advances have been incorporated.

Key historical research which has contributed to modern practice can be categorised into two distinct fields: The measurement of emotion and the therapeutic relationship. Significant current research includes studies of Jungian psychotherapy with implications for the WAE/WAT. Future research is noted separately.

Discussion of other Word Association Tests (for example, Kent & Rosanoff 1910 and the subsequent Minnesota norms) is beyond the scope of his manual.

Measurement of emotion

As noted in the first chapter, Jung's Association Experiment was not based only on word associations but also on the observation and measurement of physiological responses. The measurement of emotion has continued to be of scientific interest to date. Of particular note is Jung's use of the galvanometer (see glossary). A British experimenter, Whately Smith (1922), studied Jung's experiments and formed the opinion that the PRT was the most reliable complex indicator. This view is sometimes held today by practitioners, who (not unreasonably) make broad, working assumptions from an initial scan of the response times. However, after careful experimentation, Whately Smith eventually concluded that the galvanometer was the most reliable measure of emotional disturbance.

While the galvanometer is rarely used, these findings are incorporated into the WAE 50-and 100-word protocols insofar as they inform many of the other complex indicators. That is one of the clinical reasons adherence to the protocol is taken seriously in the training. The full range of complex indicators (not only those related to PRTs) is taken into account.

Although we do not generally use galvanic measurement, there is an argument that incorporating a simple modern version of this into the training might more faithfully replicate Jung's original work and help the experimenter to appreciate the relative importance of closely observing physiological changes accompanying client's reactions to stimulus words.

While galvanic skin response measurement (GSR) more recently found its therapeutic position in biofeedback therapies, notably in the work of Cade and Coxhead (1979), it is not generally used in the psychotherapeutic training or practice of the WAE. This is partly because of the historical complexity of setting up the experimental apparatus. However, because nowadays small GSR biofeedback instruments are readily available and can be used by applying a simple contact to the hand to produce precise real-time and recorded graphs via a laptop, there is no good reason why it should not be used for training, research or where appropriate, for clinical purposes (for example, to show that emotions are real and measurable). The use of the instrument in therapeutic practice is subject to the codes of ethics of the relevant training body and professional association (such as the United Kingdom Council for Psychotherapy). From time to time, as qualified practitioners we have used the GSR in analytic leadership coaching and consulting, either as a stand-alone or in combination with a focused WAT, and on occasion we have given the instrument to clients for personal subsequent use to identify stress and to manage stressors, in line with their preferred habitual practice.

With the growth of digital technology, there is now a broad range of (health and sports) measurement apparatus available, for example for electrical skin resistance, heart rate, temperature and brain wave activity, and if thought desirable, it would be a simple matter to incorporate this as an optional element of WAT training.

More recent scientific research into the neuropsychology of complexes (emotional clusters evoked in response to word stimuli in the WAT) is well established and described in detail by Escamilla (2021), a CGIZ graduate who ran clinical fMRI research projects in the United States, in parallel with Petchkovsky et al. (2013) in Australia. In the sense that emotional reactions are empirically observable by test instruments, this to some extent echoes Jung's seminal research using the instruments available to him at that time.

The measurement of emotion is especially relevant to pre–ego formation disturbances. Pre-verbal emotional imprints and patterns of early infancy or 'representations of interactions which have been generalised' (RIGS; Stern 1985) and which are not remembered cognitively can often be discerned in the analytic encounter through the reporting and observation and clients feeling the counter-transference. The body remembers and directs emotionally, and this may frequently be at odds with the post–ego formation cognitive knowledge and values of the client. Thus the contribution of the WAT to bridging the two worlds might go slowly or quickly depending upon the dynamic between pre– and post–ego formation, and caution is advised.

The potential benefits of integration suggested here invite further exploration of the most intransigent mental disorders, such as those which inspired Jung's original work. The suggestion resonates with Winnicott's (1956) description of the aetiology (i.e. the cause, set of causes, or manner of causation of a disease or condition) of non/organic psychosis and schizophrenia related to early environmental conditions.

It is perhaps worth pausing to include a note of behavioural approaches to the measurement of emotion which chime with Jung's complex theory. Nickerson (2023) describes the progression of theoretical understandings of emotion from William James and Lange through to Damasio et al. (1996). Damasio is credited as the author of the 'second major theory of emotion influenced by James-Lange'. These are offered here as modern interdisciplinary evidence of support for Jung's complex theory and WAT findings. In a nutshell, continuities of Jung's theory of complexes are evident in Damasio's proposal of 'somatic markers', which Nickerson describes as

> physiological reactions tied to past emotional events. New events trigger these somatic markers and influence how people make decisions. For example, someone who has had past positive experiences with dogs (for example, a dog person to, say, pet the next dog that they see).
> (2023)

Damasio has shown not only how emotions affect rational decision-making (more than is generally accepted) but also that conscious rational processes can also be brought to bear once the emotional elements have been recognised. This is consistent with our observations of the development of consciousness in response to the WAE, where both pleasant and unpleasant feeling-toned memory clusters are identified, and their effects on thinking and behaviour become available for reflection. Here it should be noted that Damasio's work implies the possibility of empirical investigation to validate the predictive validity of the WAT. In Jungian terms, the complex can indicate future decisions and behaviours. Damasio focuses on the 'normal' reality distortions of everyday life. Those taking the form of optimistic biases are frequently overlooked by analysts who are accustomed to dealing with complexes (such as a negative parent complex) arising from unpleasant experiences. Both categories of complex autonomously contribute to the client's future behaviour and experiences, and even 'positive complexes' can be problematic. For example, Nickerson's 'dog person' might lack caution in approaching a dog and be bitten. Both negative and positive complexes are, by definition, autonomous.

Even the process of rational decision-making is not as straightforward as it might sound. In fact, in many cases, it can be driven by feeling-toned complexes. For example, the unconscious defense of rationalisation is considered a thinking process largely driven by unconscious factors.

In summary, it is important for the experimenter to observe the importance of emotional measurement by taking into account all the complex indicators, such as various forms of body language, and not attempt a shortcut by over-reliance on the prolonged reaction times. The WWAE protocol template was designed with this in mind.

Humanistic and general psychotherapy

Carl Rogers

Many elementary psychotherapy skills which are taken for granted today and which are integral to delivering the WAE/WAT derive from the humanistic work, focusing on self-actualisation of Carl Rogers (1959), whose approach to clinical practice reflected much of the work of Edith Stein (1916) on empathy, and of Husserl (1950) on inter-subjectivity (see Glossary).

We concur with Fierro (2023), who notes that Rogers suffered 'obliteration by incorporation' because his work is so commonly accepted that it is rarely cited. Nonetheless, to ensure that these important elements in general psychotherapy are firmly incorporated into the WWAE training, we have taken the precaution of making them explicit. They include self-actualisation, empathy, congruency and unconditional positive regard. A key skill is reflective listening, evidenced by summaries and reflections made in genuine attempts to understand the client and to foster a safe learning environment to stimulate further self-exploration. These skills are especially helpful when conducting the WAE/WAT context interview. In this latter regard, sharing a transcript after the context interview provides useful content reflection prior to a deeper feedback discussion, thus continuing to build psychological safety and trust between the experimenter and the client. It is interesting to note that inspired by Jung, Rogers's early work included his own 'unsuccessful word association experiments with children' (Fierro 2023).

Wampold

The humanist, client-centred perspective in general psychotherapy was significantly strengthened by the research of Wampold and Imel (2015), who made an extensive meta-study of the common factors contributing to the efficacy and effectiveness of psychotherapy. Wampold concluded that the humanistic relationship factors, such as alliance, empathy, expectations, cultural adaptation and therapist differences (contextual model factors), outweigh by far the factors relating to psychotherapy technique or adherence to any particular school. His presentation of the factors also shows where results were supported by RCTs (randomised control trials) and EBTs (evidence-based treatments).

The findings are especially relevant to the WAE/WAT training, where we have placed emphasis on the big levers of empathy and the working alliance. These factors take on even greater significance in clinical practice, where the experimenter is also the analyst providing continuing therapy.

In a later commentary on these results, Elkins (2022) states that 'the human and relational elements are potent agents of change' and that 'In fact, they are the "powerhouse" of effective therapy and without those elements, therapy could not work'.

Freese (2024) explains the relevance of this to the workplace:

> Employee Engagement Surveys – these humanistic relationship factors are measured too, and in that context, results show time and again the importance for employees' feelings of motivation, belonging and loyalty to the organisation deliver greater satisfaction and enjoyment of efficient and mutually productive work.

The authors concur that when the WAE is described as a 'test' in training, this militates against the building of an optimal real relationship because it introduces an association of power distance between the experimenter and the client. It is fairly obvious that in cases where clients come to the experiment with prior bad learning experiences, these will sometimes show up as complexes. According to Jung, if a cluster of such emotionally charged memories predominates the experiment, then a response is categorised as a 'complex-constellation type' (CW 2, para. 149). However, if the boundary conditions of the experiment are presented in a 'test-like' manner ('teacher' tone of voice, classroom setting and rigid presenter), then regardless of the neutrality of the stimulus words, the relationship and setting are likely to evoke 'bad learning' associations in clients who, in a more relaxed and neutral setting, would not exhibit the complex. (Thus the boundary conditions, which include the experimenter skill of putting the client at ease, can be thought of as a confounding variable.)

This can be taken into account by triangulating evidence in the following ways.

1 The unconscious perceptions of the boundary conditions of the experiment including the experimenter are usually expressed in derivative feedback (Casement 1985; Langs 1992). This is a form of encoded associative narrative through which the client communicates their unconscious views of the experimenter and the boundary conditions known, although (by definition) they are not consciously aware of them at that moment. For example, when

commenting about their experience after completing the protocol, clients might say, 'It was all fine. There were no problems. I am usually OK with tests, but I remember that my chemistry teacher was really uptight and she made us all terrified. Maybe she was a new teacher'. This is partly why we encourage experimenters to seek casual feedback when the protocol has been completed.

2 An exploration of experimenter counter-transference in their own supervision can help to differentiate experimenter 'bad learning' complexes from those of the client.

These two methods are not mutually exclusive. Individual complexes are constellated in the bi-personal field of the therapeutic encounter. However, it should be noted that the natural tendency of the experimenter is to overlook critical derivative feedback commenting on boundary violations, especially as they reveal experimenter complexes.

Subtle considerations such as these improve the validity of the experiment (see Glossary).

From the humanist perspective it can be seen that the healing process is essentially relational and not only psychodynamic but also psycho-social. Training in the WAE/WAT is informed by person-centred psychotherapy. From our Jungian perspective, this engagement of two people in an experiment dealing with the conscious and the unconscious invites the transcendent function through the juxtaposition and dialogue of what is scientifically known and the unconscious realms of the psyche. Symbols of transformation and archetypes appear, evidencing the individuation process. This latter point is beyond the scope of this volume but is described as a separate topic by Kast (1992).

Common factor models in psychotherapy research

In the humanist tradition, focus on relationship in the therapeutic encounter informed a broader trend of looking at common factors in different modes of psychotherapy rather than focusing on the different competing schools. This included a shift away from manualised treatments focusing on specific disorders towards trans-diagnostic and modular treatment methods which address the common core aspects of similar classes of diagnoses such as anxiety disorders that are associated with a high risk of comorbidity, i.e. the simultaneous presence of two or more diseases or medical conditions in a patient.

> This approach could be particularly suited to psycho-dynamic psychotherapy, because it is traditionally less tailored to the symptoms of single mental disorders, rather than problems, especially in the relational sphere, that are common to many mental conditions, and promotes a dimensional model of classification focusing on the core underlying processes of mental conditions.
>
> (Yakeley 2018, p. 5)

WAT research lends itself well both to the diagnosis of certain disorders and to the relational common factors underlying similar classes. Yakeley (2018) reports that this has already been applied to major depressive disorders and to post-traumatic stress disorders. The WAT identifies complexes, which (from a developmental point of view (Stern 1985) derive from representations of interactions which have been generalised (RIGS). In clinical practice, it is not too difficult to identify common factors for more serious disorders with pre-ego aetiology (before c. 3 years old) such as infant relational disturbances, neglect or abuse. As these emerge, the underlying archetypal images and stories indicate potential paths to health (see Chapters 7–9).

In the WWAE/WAT it is quite acceptable to give an interpretation hypothesis based on common factors. An example would be early deprivation and abuse.

Current WAE/WAT research approaches

A landmark in empirical research into Jungian psychotherapy was reached in 2013, when Roesler demonstrated that 'Jungian psychotherapy has reached the point where it can be called an empirically proven, effective method' (Roesler 2013, p. 562).

Roesler gives a detailed explanation of how the WAT can be used in pre-post outcome design in combination with diverse combinations of empirical measurement instruments used to investigate the efficacy and effectiveness of psycho-dynamic therapies. It is most helpful that he has provided not only suggestions for the improvement of the measurement of efficacy but also blueprint designs for RTCs. The WAT lends itself well to the identification of the changing structure of complexes over the course of therapy, for example, the differentiation of the ego complex from the parental complexes. (We have also found it instrumental in the further differentiation from both trans-generational and cultural complexes.) We expect to see further incorporation of Roesler's research approach into the training and practice of Jungian psychotherapy and particularly the WAE and the WAT.

For example, by using mixed research methods, Roesler appears to have enabled a step towards the use of the WAT as an adjunct to standard and psycho-dynamic diagnostic and therapy outcome measures for particular disorders, such as for unipolar depression.

From analytical psychology itself, type psychology and symbols of transformation (which can show landmark indicators of the individuation journey) can be observed during the WAE, and this is a current topic of research interest (Roesler 2013).

Artificial intelligence (AI)

Potential further developments in the WAE are being stimulated by the growth of artificial intelligence (AI). For some time, there have been IT-based models which can help with the calculations, graphs and tables involved in the WAT. These include models developed by O'Brien (2021). (The software is available to qualified practitioners upon request at cgjungcentre.com.) We do not recommend that these instruments are used in WAE training, but they can be useful for experienced experimenters who need to improve the efficiency of desk time.

However, AI now promises potential new developments in the analysis of the word association part of the experiment. These are based on associative memory networks (AMNs). Associative memory networks are engendering significant developments in artificial intelligence, and they are described as neural networks, modeled on the neural nodes and synapses in the human brain. In fact, this is what a complex map looks like. There is a strong resemblance between this approach and the one implicitly used by Kast (1980) in her instructions for the mapping of complexes.

Shono et al. (2016) describe AMNs as follows: 'Associative network models posit that concepts are represented in an associative memory network as nodes, which are interconnected among one another through links with varying levels of associative strength'. It is argued that the AMN reveals 'memory activation patterns' which 'reflect one's repetitive experiences in everyday life'. This is (so far) crudely modeled on understandings of neuropsychology and appears to support Jung's complex theory.

A simple view of AI (Witkowski and Ward 2020) describes four neuron layers: Inputs, associations, outputs, and feedback. 'These layers are analogous to the human brain in the following respects. The input layer receives stimulation from the outside world and transforms it into signals for further processing'.

In the associative layer, there is a process of pattern recognition, where connections are made between input patterns and patterns stored in the memory.

The output layer retrieves the patterns and gives an output, and the feedback layer stimulates learning whereby associations are adjusted and performance is involved. This is analogous to the process of human adjustment and adaptation, or reality orientation, failures of which give rise to psychological disorders.

Of particular interest are machine learning models such as the Hopfield model and the Boltzman machine, where every node is connected to every other node, whether visible or hidden, to create a system of pattern recognition and learning without labels to reveal deeper levels of organisation (Marullo & Agliari 2020). In this respect, the models appeal as methods of exploring deeper layers of Association in the WAE/WAT.

This overview is sufficient to demonstrate the first-level similarities between Jung's Word Association Experiment (and complex theory) and artificial intelligence. A more detailed survey of the AI field is provided by Oludare and Aman (2018), in which the perspectives on deeper fields appear analogous to the approach to the deep unconscious as described by Jung.

Clinical implications

Both in the context interview and therapy following the WWAE, it can be helpful to encourage the patient to discover some of the 'horizontal' associations.

Here I make working definitions to differentiate between vertical and horizontal chains of association. Vertical chains are those made in response to a stimulus word until the associations cease (e.g. Tennis elbow foot etc.). Horizontal chains are those which are subsequently made between response words. For example, another vertical chain might be (Water, river, bend etc.).

A horizontal association (of shared meaning) might be elbow/bend.

This can naturally happen, for example, when tracing the connections between stereotypes. Furthermore, there is an interesting coincidence in the deepening progression of the exploration of associative memory networks and the emergence of psychological phenomena which operate across time and space boundaries. This seems to be recursive in the microbiology of the brain as the proteins at the heart of neurons (micro-tubules) exhibit quantum behaviour.

Regardless of these avenues of potential further research, one practical finding from our practice is that a recursion of the complex interview method based purely on word association (as described in Appendix 1) can deliver improved understanding and therapeutic benefit. It would be possible to develop a prototype for such a repeated application to coding and association rules.

Reflections

The Word Association Test has been a research topic of much debate between experimental researchers and clinical practitioners since its publication in the early 1900s (1906–1909). The discussion has been somewhat paradigmatic of Jung's opus, which, beginning with his experimental researches and the WAT, quickly grew to include exploration of the deep individual and collective unconscious. With its parallels in the evolution of other fields of enquiry ranging from physics to the social science, the practice of analytical psychology is an exploration and facilitation of the relationship between measurable behaviors and the minimally known and immeasurably vast realms of the human psyche. This exploration expands awareness of consciousness and supports individuation, the natural drive of the psyche towards wholeness. It is a lifelong process which embraces differentiation between the conscious and unconscious and a holding of the tension of opposites which leads to an unknown third in the form of a symbol ('*tertium non datur*'; see glossary). Autonomous split-off elements are incorporated, and re-enactment is reduced. The tendency is towards union. Starting with empirical measurement and progressing towards awareness of complexes and the underlying archetypes, the WAE/WAT training serves this purpose well. It familiarises candidates with diverse but complementary fields of human enquiry while stimulating the personal development required to become a Jungian analyst.

As we proceed to consider research matters, to incorporate research into practice and to build research/practitioner models, we offer the reminder that in both training and clinical use, the WAT is used to raise consciousness of complexes which inform the development of the whole character through the journey of individuation. Jung had discovered that the WAT unfolded a hidden and living emotional landscape infused with the totality of the life experiences of the client, and while not a test in the terms he has originally conceived, he nonetheless delivered a protocol which is now proving to have been far ahead of its time in delivering felt and measurable psychotherapeutic value.

References

Cade, M, Coxhead, N 1979, *The Awakened Mind: Biofeedback and Development of Higher States of Awareness*, Element Books, London.

Casement, P 1985, *On Learning from the Patient*, Tavistock Publications, London.

Damasio, A, Everitt, J, Bishop, D 1996, 'The Somatic marker hypothesis and the possible functions of the Prefrontal Cortex', *Biological Sciences*, vol. 351, pp. 1413–1420, <www.jstor.org/stable/3069187>.

Elkins, D 2022, 'Common factors: What are they and what do they mean for humanistic psychology?', *Journal of Humanistic Psychology*, vol. 62, no. 1, pp. 21–30.

Escamilla, M 2021, 'Neuroscience and Jung', In O'Brien, N & O'Brien, J (Eds.), *The Professional Practice of Jungian Coaching*, Routledge, London & New York.

Fierro, C 2023, 'A supposedly objective thing I'll never use again: Word association and the quest for validity and reliability in emotional adjustment research from Carl Jung to Carl Rogers (1898– 1927)', *Journal of the History of the Behavioural Science*, vol. 60, no. 1, <doi: 10.1002/jhbs.22272>.

Freese, H 2004, *Editorial Correspondence*, February 28, 2024.

Husserl, E 1950, *Cartesian Meditations*, Husserliana: Edmunt Husserl: Collected works, vol. 1, Springer, New York.

Jung, CG 1904–7/1910, *Experimental Researches*, CW 2.

Jung, CG 2000, *The Collected Works of C. G. Jung* (CW), eds. H Read, M Fordham, G Adler and W McGuire, trans. RFC Hull, Princeton University Press, Princeton.

Jung, CG 2012, *The Red Book*, ed. Sonu Sahmdasani, W. W. Norton Company, New York.

Jung, CG 2020, *The Black Books*, ed. Sonu Sahmdasani, W. W. Norton Company, New York.

Kast, V 1980, *Excerpts in English from 'Das assoziationsexperiment in der therapeutischen praxis'*, trans. Irene Gad, Bonz Verlag, Fellback-Oeffingen.

Kast, V 1992, *The Dynamics of Symbols: Fundamentals of Jungian Psychotherapy*, Fromm Intl., New York.

Kent, H, Rosanoff, J 1910, 'A study of association in insanity', *American Journal of Insanity*, vol. 67, pp. 37–96.

Langs, R 1992, *A Clinical Workbook for Psychotherapists*, Karnac Books, London.

Marullo, C, Agliari E 2020, 'Boltzmann machines as generalized hopfield networks: A review of recent results and outlooks', *Entropy*, vol. 29, no. 23, <doi: 10.3390/e23010034. PMID: 33383716; PMCID: PMC7823871>.

Nickerson, C 2023, 'James-Lange theory of emotion: Definition and examples'. viewed 21 February 2024, <www.simplypsychology.org/what-is-the-james-lange-theory-of-emotion.html>.

Oludare, A, Aman, J 2018, *State-of-the-Art in Artificial Neural Network Applications: A Survey*, Helyon, Elsevier.

Petchkovsky, L, Petchkovsky, M, Morris, P, Dickson, P, Montgomery, D, Dwyer, J, Burnett, P 2013, 'fMRI responses to Jung's Word Association Test: Implications for theory, treatment and research', *Journal of Analytical Psychology*, vol. 58, no. 3, pp. 409–431, <doi: 10.1111/1468-5922.12021. PMID: 23750943>.

Roesler, C 2013, 'Evidence for the effectiveness of Jungian psychotherapy: A review of empirical studies', *Behavioural Science*, vol. 3, no. 4, pp. 562–575, <doi: 10.3390/bs3040562. PMID: 25379256; PMCID: PMC4217606>.

Rogers, C 1959, *A Theory of Therapy, Personality, and Interpersonal Relationships: As Developed in the Client-Centered Framework*, McGraw-Hill, New York.

Shono, Y, Ames, S, Stacy, A 2016, 'Evaluation of internal validity using modern test theory: Application to word association', *Psychological Assessment*, vol. 28, no. 2, pp. 194–204, <doi: 10.1037/pas0000175>.

Smith, W 1922, *The Measurement of Emotion*. Harcourt Brace & Company, San Francisco.

Stein, E 1916, On the Problem of Empathy, ICS, LA.

Stern, D 1985, *The Interpersonal World of the Infant*, Basic Books, New York.

Szanto, T, Dermot, M 2020, 'Edith Stein', *The Stanford Encyclopedia of Philosophy*. Metaphysics Research Lab Philosophy Department Stanford University Stanford, CA 94305. Visited February 12, <https://plato.stanford.edu/archives/spr2020/entries/stein/>.

Wampold, B, Imel, Z 2015, *The Great Psychotherapy Debate: The Evidence for What Makes Psychotherapy Work*, Routledge, New York.

Winnicott, D 1956, *Collected Papers*, Tavistock Clinic, London.

Witkowski, J, Ward, T 2020, *Artificial Intelligence in Healthcare*, pp. 179–202, Academic Press, Cambridge.

Yakeley, J 2018, 'Jessica psychodynamic psychotherapy: Developing the evidence base, Advances in Psychiatric Treatment', vol. 20, no. 4, pp. 269–279, <doi: 10.1192/apt.bp.113.01>.

13 Further thoughts

John O'Brien

Jung's opus as context for the Word Association Experiment

Jung's interest in a scientific research approach to understanding the human psyche in general, and to mental illness in particular, was apparent in the Zofingia lectures (five lectures) which he gave over a period of four years (1896 to 1899) while a member of the Zofingia Society (the Zofingiaverein) a multi-university fraternity (of which his father had been a member) and while studying at the Medical School of Basel University, not far from the church where his father was a minister. His professional commitment to a scientific (empirical) approach to psychological and spiritual phenomena drew criticism from his fellows as being 'mystic'. From the position of a scientist, Jung strove to investigate subjective phenomena from a scientific standpoint. This enquiry became the central *leitmotif* (recurrent and recursive theme) of his opus. Notably, in his May 1897 lecture he stated:

> In research we are completely dependent on the empirical method ***and*** The soul is independent of space and time.

It is not difficult to imagine the potential developmental origins of this effort, as from early childhood he had struggled to make sense of his family and social circumstances, having been born in 1875 in a religious family, exposed to sexual abuse (Maguire) and living through two world wars. In his final work, *Mysterium Coniunctionis*, completed in 1970 when he was 80 years old, and five years before his death, Jung shows the dynamic relationship between the tensions of opposites. With reference to alchemical symbolism, Jung notes how these are transcended in specific stages, in a series of differentiation and unions within the context of progression towards a greater union. This can be considered an illustration of how, over a lifetime, and at moments along the way, the tendency to think in binary terms gives way to a holistic experience and an appreciation (in Jungian terms, of individuation).

> The factors which come together in the coniunctio are conceived as opposites, either confronting one another in enmity or attracting one another in love. To begin with they form a dualism; for instance the opposites are *humidum* (moist)/*siccum* (dry), *frigidum* (cold)/*calidum* (warm), *superior* (upper, higher)/*inferior* (lower), *spiritus-anima* (spirit-soul)/*corpus* (body), *coelum* (heaven)/*terra* (earth), *ignis* (fire)/*aqua* (water), bright/dark, *agens* (active)/*patiens* (passive), *volatile* (volatile, gaseous)/*fixum* (solid), *pretiosum* (precious, costly; also *carum*, dear)/vile (cheap, common), *bonum* (good)/*malum* (evil), *manifestum* (open)/*occultum* (occult; also *celatum*, hidden), *oriens* (East)/*occidens* (West),

vivum (living)/*mortuum* (dead). Often the polarity is arranged as a quaternio (quaternity), with the two opposites crossing one another, as for instance the four elements or the four qualities (moist, dry, cold, warm), or the four directions and seasons, thus producing the cross as an emblem of the four elements and symbol of the sublunary physical world.

(CW 14, para. 1)

The implicit theme in this paragraph is the *leitmotif* which comprises the main chapters of *Mysterium Coniunctionis* (CW 14, para. 970):

I The components of the coniunction
II The paradoxa
III The personification of the opposites
IV Rex and regina
V Adam and Eve
VI The conjunction
VII Epilogue

The shape of the process of individuation can be seen from the chapter titles, as each chapter contains the core theme of the progressive separation and union of opposites while also representing a specific stage in within the whole volume which itself represents that theme. This shape can be termed 'fractal'.

Having noted his first and last publications, from a fractal perspective it seems fitting to consider not only the opening chapter of *Mysterium Coniunctionis* (CW 14) but also the last chapter of that volume, in which Jung writes:

Alchemy, with its wealth of symbols, gives us an insight into an endeavour of the human mind which could be compared with a religious rite, an opus divinum. The difference between them is that the alchemical opus was not a collective activity rigorously defined as to its form and content, but rather, despite the similarity of their fundamental principles, an individual undertaking on which the adept staked his whole soul for the transcendental purpose of producing a unity. It was a work of reconciliation between apparently incompatible opposites, which, characteristically, were understood not merely as the natural hostility of the physical elements but at the same time as a moral conflict.

(CW 14, para. 90)

Here, Jung gingerly notes the similar if not common principles of individuation in the collective and the group (albeit expressed in alchemical allegory and symbolism). Furthermore, and somewhat conclusively, he states:

Since the object of this endeavour was seen outside as well as inside, as both physical and psychic, the work extended as it were through the whole of nature, and its goal consisted in a symbol which had an empirical and at the same time a transcendental aspect.

(CW 14, para. 90)

This last sentence is critical in that it seems as though he regards the principles universal intrinsic to the 'whole of nature', operating in both the separate and unified system domains of physical and psychic.

From a psychological perspective, the principle is discernible in the process of individuation, the journey of the psyche towards wholeness containing the differentiation and union which are also characteristic of the journey seen as a whole. Thus the characteristics of the micro level are observable at the macro level.

From a physics perspective the principle is discernible in the progression from 'objective' science to participant/observer approaches to quantum theory to the concept of the *unus mundus* (one world). This is implicit in 'Synchronicity an acausal connecting principle' and explicit in 'Structure and dynamics of the psyche' (CW 8), *Mysterium Coniunctionis* (CW 14) and in Jung's correspondence with Wolfgang Pauli (Atom and Archetype).

For example:

> Undoubtedly the idea of the *unus mundus* is founded on the assumption that the multiplicity of the empirical world rests on an underlying unity, and that not two or more fundamentally different worlds exist side by side or are mingled with one another. Rather, everything divided and different belongs to one and the same world, which is not the world of sense but a postulate whose probability is vouched for by the fact that until now no one has been able to discover a world in which the known laws of nature are invalid. That even the psychic world, which is so extraordinarily different from the physical world, does not have its roots outside the one cosmos is evident from the undeniable fact that causal connections exist between the psyche and the body which point to their underlying unitary nature.
>
> (CW 14, para. 767)

Reference to individual parts of Jung's work without an appreciation of the whole opus can sometimes make it difficult to follow the logic of his arguments because he sometimes writes in an associative style. In this regard his medium is his message, and the persevering reader may absorb the meaning as much by 'osmosis' and their own stimulated associations as by binary thinking and deductive logic. As with Jung's work itself, over time, the tension between the opposite styles of learning produces a unified whole. In a manner similar to the appreciation of sacred scriptures, deeper understandings emerge as the reader develops through the life stages.

From a phenomenological perspective, binary thinking might appear concretely useful but accompanied by a danger of splitting and paranoia. From a binary thinking perspective, the *unus mundus* might appear mystical 'hocus pocus'. As in sacred scriptures: Allegories, paradoxes and symbols (with their numinous attraction) bridge the divide; CW 5.

The fractal quality of Jung's approach

Having given a brief overview of Jung's opus, perhaps the unifying fractal quality (necessarily involving recursion) can now be more clearly observed. For the purposes of this volume, I use a modified version of the standard definition (Merriam Webster) of 'fractal' as follows:

> any of various [elements] for which any suitably chosen part is similar in shape to a given larger or smaller part when magnified or reduced to the same size.

Simply put, a viewing of Jung's work through a fractal lens (which, like a microscope or telescope, offers different views of the same dynamic recursions across temporal and spatial boundaries) reveals the essential *leitmotif*. Furthermore, the viewing of his work in this way is implicitly suggested in work (Q.E.D.). A mathematical example can be found in the Mandlebrot set (1983; 2004). If the fractal hypothesis is correct, then we would expect it to be applicable across many domains and in particular to further inform the analytic associative process. For reference, the closest contemporary resonant work is 'A Fractal Epistemology for a Scientific Psychology: Bridging the Personal with the Transpersonal' (Marks-Tarlow et al. 2020).

An elaboration of artificial intelligence

Artificial intelligence (ChatGPT-4) informs us that

> Associations in the brain are fundamental to understanding how information is processed, stored, and retrieved. In psychology and neuroscience, associations refer to the connections formed between different elements of information, such as thoughts, experiences, or stimuli. These connections enable the brain to make sense of the world, learn from past experiences, and adapt to new situations.
>
> (ChatGPT-4, 2024)

It is most interesting to note the peculiar nature of this last paragraph, as it was produced by ChatGPT-4, an artificial intelligence system modeled on neural networks, which in turn are modeled upon the known structural and informational systems of the human brain. I use the word 'known' quite deliberately to imply the connotation that in comparison to what is still unknown, our existing state of scientific knowledge seems both precious and little.

The curious reader might notice that the structure of the above ideas is fractal and recursive, i.e. that the phenomenon of brain networks has been described by a model designed by a human brain through a medium modeled on the observed brain. This implicit structure (thematically similar layers within layers) is the fractal quality strikingly implicit in Jung's opus and provides not only a valuable context for a full appreciation of the Word Association Experiment but also a fundamental means of a modern understanding of the psychology and neuroscience of associations.

An elaboration of neuroscience and psychiatry

An examination of Jung's ideas and scientific observations of the associative relationship between the conscious and unconscious, and between thinking and emotion seems to be similar in shape (isomorphic) to modern neuro-scientific network theories and observations. As explained in Chapter 12, the human brain makes associations through synapses and neurons.

According to Caire et al. (2024),

> The human brain is made up of approximately 86 billion neurons that 'talk' to each other using a combination of electrical and chemical (electrochemical) signals. The places where neurons connect and communicate with each other are called synapses. Each neuron has anywhere between a few to hundreds of thousands of synaptic connections, and these connections can be with itself, neighboring neurons, or neurons in other regions of the brain. A synapse is made up of a presynaptic and postsynaptic terminal.
>
> The presynaptic terminal is at the end of an axon and is the place where the electrical signal (the action potential) is converted into a chemical signal (neurotransmitter release). The postsynaptic terminal membrane is less than 50 nanometers away and contains specialized receptors. The neurotransmitter rapidly (in microseconds) diffuses across the synaptic cleft and binds to specific receptors.

The type of neurotransmitter released from the presynaptic terminal and the specific receptors present on the corresponding postsynaptic terminal is critical in determining the quality and intensity of information transmitted by neurons. The postsynaptic neuron integrates all the signals it receives to determine what it does next, for example, to fire an action potential of its own or not.

In Chapter 12 we noted the similarity between these networks, neural networks and the complex mapping process used by Kast (1980) in her description of the Word Association Experiment. It could reasonably be said that neural networks are to some extent fractal representations of cognitive functioning.

But we do not live by brain alone. The brain is not the whole body. What is special about the Word Association Experiment is that it also takes into account emotions, which are still scientifically mysterious as well as being simply observable and measurable. This is elegantly depicted in Kast's method of complex mapping.

In the Word Association Experiment, it is not only the fine relationship between emotions which is depicted but also the temporal relationship between past, present and future and the spatial relationship between individual, group and global phenomena.

As we start to consider more complex areas of neuroscience and particularly brain structure, it is perhaps worth noting the key regions of the brain associated with emotional processing.

According to Sadock and Sadok (2007, p. 89) the boundaries of the limbic system were first delineated by Papez (1937) as follows: Hippocampus, fornix, mamillary bodies, anterior nucleus of the thalamus and cingulate gyrus (Sadock and Kaplan, 2007) and subsequently expanded to include the amygdala, septum, basal forebrain, nucleus accumbens and orbitofrontal cortex.

Functional definitions of the amygdala, the prefrontal cortex, the anterior cingulate cortex, the insula, the hippocampus, the basal ganglia and the hypothalamus are provided in what follows (adapted from Šimić et al. 2021):

Amygdala: The amygdala is perhaps the most well-known brain structure associated with emotional processing. It is involved in the detection and processing of emotions, particularly fear and threat-related stimuli. The amygdala plays a crucial role in the generation of emotional responses and the modulation of emotional memories.

Prefrontal cortex (PFC): The prefrontal cortex, particularly the ventromedial prefrontal cortex (vmPFC) and the orbitofrontal cortex (OFC), is involved in emotion regulation and decision-making. These regions help regulate emotional responses, inhibit inappropriate emotional reactions and integrate emotional information with higher cognitive processes.

Anterior cingulate cortex (ACC): The anterior cingulate cortex is implicated in various aspects of emotional processing, including emotion regulation, conflict monitoring and pain perception. It plays a role in detecting emotional conflicts and adjusting behavior accordingly.

Insula: The insular cortex is involved in the subjective experience of emotions, including interoceptive awareness (sensing internal bodily states) and the representation of emotional feelings. It helps integrate sensory and emotional information and plays a role in empathy and social emotions.

Hippocampus: While primarily known for its role in memory formation, the hippocampus also contributes to emotional processing by encoding and retrieving emotional memories. It interacts with the amygdala to consolidate emotionally significant events into long-term memory.

Basal ganglia: The basal ganglia, including structures like the nucleus accumbens and the ventral striatum, are involved in reward processing and motivation. They play a role in the experience of pleasure, reinforcement learning and the regulation of motivated behaviors.

Hypothalamus: The hypothalamus serves as a key interface between the brain and the body's physiological responses to emotion. It regulates autonomic functions (e.g. heart rate, blood pressure) and endocrine responses (e.g. stress hormones) associated with emotional arousal.

These brain regions form interconnected networks that enable the complex processing of emotional information, including the perception, interpretation, and regulation of emotions. Dysfunction in these areas can lead to various emotional disorders, such as anxiety disorders, depression and post-traumatic stress disorder (PTSD).

A closer look at features of the limbic system is most interesting in view of the fractal nature of the Word Association and its applications.

> Emotion plays a very important role in our daily lives, affecting our social interactions, with more than 80–90% of human psychological problems being emotional problems. However, emotion is considered to be one of the earliest studied but least known subjects among all life sciences.
>
> (Wang et al. 2020)

According to Wang et al. (2020), the limbic system model described here was, until the mid-20th century, an accepted way of describing the connection between the human brain and emotions. Since that time, research focus has shifted from discrete organic locations in the brain to neurotransmitters and hormones, which describe the chemical means by which signals are transmitted around and beyond the limbic system. This is partly because emotions are processed to different extents and in diverse and combinations by the various centres. (The research is largely focused on major depressive disorder.)

Jiang et al. (2022) helpfully refer to a range of related research including the brain–gut axis and the brain–liver axis as well as neuroplasticity.

While maintaining a sound scientific focus on the chemical mechanisms and including further research thereby derived, Jiang et al also take into account developmental environmental and, epidemiological factors.

This has all the logical indicators of movement towards a holistic approach to the human psyche, the human brain and the human being with various facets, darkly and dimly lit as far as our knowledge and wonder are capable.

If one final piece of evidence is to be cited, then Jung et al. (2016) provide sound evidence that within the human brain, the structural connectivity of higher-order association cortices reflects human functional brain networks in a particular manner.

> Human higher cognition arises from the main tertiary association cortices including the frontal, temporal and parietal lobes. Many studies have suggested that cortical functions must be shaped or emerge from the pattern of underlying physical (white matter) connectivity . . .
>
> Using graph-theory network analysis we revealed five physically-connected sub-networks, which correspond directly to five known functional networks. This study provides strong and direct evidence that core functional brain networks mirror the brain's structural connectivity.
>
> (Jung et al. 2016)

An elaboration of connection and interpretation derived from the Word Association Experiment

The patient experience is one of making connections on the journey to appreciating the whole. It is the experimenter journey too.

In the various chapters of this manual, each procedural part of the Word Association Experiment has been made explicit, and their relevance to the whole has been demonstrated. The protocol is clear and can be followed in a linear fashion. At the same time it contains a fractal quality which embraces both appreciation of logical enquiry and a call to explore the mysterious domains into which we are invited via the numinous symbols which are constellated in images: Words, sounds, pictures, feelings; in fact, through all the senses of both the experimenter and client which give rise to the numinous symbols which call us onwards. We have seen perhaps that the whole story is permeated by a deeper mystery which appears in fractal form, or maybe this is still yet to be discovered by the reader.

There is much more of value to be examined in Jung's early experimental work which has not been detailed in this manual. For example, his classification of associations, while having been gently touched upon, is worthy of deeper consideration for incorporation into advanced manuals. For reference, Jung provides a detailed list and summary of these in CW 2 (paras. 29–110) and in the summary in CW 2 (paras. 111–113).

There is also his enduring enquiry into schizophrenia, a topic which unfortunately must be left largely unexplored in this manual. However, as it is where Jung started, it seem fitting to note that there is still a great deal to be gained as informed and well-intended discussions between analytical psychology and psychiatry continue to this day (for example Howe & Demjaha 2022), and research interest in Jung's work, and particularly in the Word Association Experiment, will drive an increasingly unified body of theory and practice to support patient well-being.

Here, Jung's family constellation theory seems relevant as does his emphasis on meaning. If we are to consider Jung's work through the fractal lenses of the telescope and the microscope, then the context and meaning of a disease appear to show essential patterns, and health is associated with shared meaning. If particular expressions are difficult to understand, that is all that they are. The deeper the connection to sources beyond our everyday discourse, the greater our responsibility to interpret our own thoughts and inner conversations and to help others to interpret and communicate theirs.

We have seen that this is most important in cases where 'meaninglessness' has contributed to diagnoses of schizophrenia. Jung was clear that for the patient, there is usually some form of meaning, and so the question is how to make it shared. Sometimes this starts with an analyst either directly with a patient or with a patient's relatives. In all cases, the fundamental connection is one of empathy. And this is perhaps what the training in the Word Association Experiment can help to teach us.

But Jung was not the first to dedicate himself to helping people connect with and interpret the messages from the Self, and it is a decidedly Jungian approach to consider how the wisdoms of the ages apply to today's individual and collective 'disorders', ranging from people diagnosed with schizophrenia to our attempts to understand the collective psychosis that is war:

> There are it may be, many voices in the world, and none of them without signification. (1 Corinthians V10)
>
> He that speaketh in an unknown tongue speaketh not unto men but unto God: For no man understandeth him; how be it in the spirit he speaketh mysteries. (1 Corinthians V11)
>
> ... pray that he may interpret (1 Corinthians V13)
>
> I will sing with my spirit, but I will also sing with my understanding. (1 Corinthians V14)

References

Caire, M, Reddy, V, Varacallo, M 2024, 'Physiology, synapse', National Library of Medicine. Visited March 12, 2024. <www.ncbi.nlm.nih.gov/books/NBK526047/>.

Jiang, Y, Zou, D, Li, Y, Gu, S, Dong, J, Ma, X, Xu, S, Wang, F, Huang, J 2022, 'Monoamine neurotransmitters control basic emotions and affect major depressive disorders', *Pharmaceuticals*, vol. 28, no. 15, pp. 1181–1203. <doi: 10.3390/ph15101203. PMID: 36297314; PMCID: PMC9611768>.

Jung, CG 1909/1984, *Zofinga Lectures*, CW A.

Jung, CG 2000, *The Collected Works of C. G. Jung* (CW), eds. H Read, M Fordham, G Adler and W McGuire, trans. RFC Hull, CWs 2, 5, 8, 14, Princeton University Press, Princeton.

Jung, J, Cloutman, L, Binney, R, Lambon, R 2016, 'The structural connectivity of higher order association cortices reflects human functional brain networks', *Cortex*, vol. 97, pp. 221–239. <doi: 10.1016/j.cortex.2016.08.011>.

Kast, V 1980, *Excerpts in English from 'Das assoziationsexperiment in der therapeutischen praxis'*, trans. Irene Gad, Bonz Verlag, Fellback-Oeffingen.

Marks-Tarlow, T, Shapiro, Y, Wolf, K, Friedman, H 2020, *A fractal epistemology for a scientific psychology: Bridging the personal with the transpersonal*, Cambridge Scholars, Cambridge. Visited March 13, 2024. <www.cambridgescholars.com/resources/pdfs/978-1-5275-4023-1-sample.pdf>.

Papez, JW 1937, 'A proposed mechanism of emotion', *Archives of Neurology & Psychiatry*, vol. 38, pp. 725–743.

Sadock, BJ, Kaplan, HI, Sadock, VA 2007, *Kaplan & Sadock's Synopsis of Psychiatry: Behavioral Sciences/Clinical Psychiatry* (10th ed.), Wolter Kluwer/Lippincott Williams & Wilkins.

Sadock, BJ, Sadock, V 2007, *Synopsis of Psychiatry*, Lippincott Williams & Wilkins, New York.

Šimić, G, Tkalčić, M, Vukić, V, Mulc, D, Španić, E, Šagud, M, Olucha-Bordonau, F, Vukšić, M, Hof, P 2021, 'Understanding emotions: Origins and roles of the amygdala', *Biomolecules*, vol. 31, no. 11, pp. 801–823. <doi: 10.3390/biom11060823>.

Wang, F, Yang, J, Pan, F, Ho, R, Huang, J 2020, 'Editorial: Neurotransmitters and emotions', *Frontiers in Psychology*, vol. 29, pp. 11–21. <doi: 10.3389/fpsyg.2020.00021>.

Glossary of terms

John O'Brien

Introduction

The glossary gives definitions of key terms found in this manual. In cases of contentious definitions, more than one source is cited. Sources are drawn directly from the *Collected Works of C.G. Jung*, from post-Jungian commentary on analytical psychology, and from clinical and general psychology. The definitions with 'best fit' in the context of the manual have been selected, and where definitions are contentious, definitions from alternative sources are given. The aim is to provide the reader with different perspectives on key terms from empirical sciences as well as from phenomenological psychotherapeutic practice, thereby communicating something of the nature of the Word Association Experiment and enabling multidisciplinary discourse. Where appropriate, the entries are accompanied by an editorial comment. For further elaboration of key terms with full contextual explanations, readers are referred to Samuels et al. (1986) and for a comprehensive synopsis of Psychiatry to Ruiz et al. (2022).

A combined subject and author index detailing items which might be of interest (such as acronyms) not listed here may be found in the combined subject and author index at the end of this volume.

Glossary

Abandonment   Desertion or substantial leave-taking by a parent or primary caregiver of their custodial and other responsibilities to a dependent. Dependents are usually children but may also be adult individuals who are ill (Vanden Bos 2007).

> Abandonment, exposure, danger, etc are all elaborations of the 'child's; insignificant beginnings and of its mysterious and miraculous birth. This statement describes a certain psychic experience of a creative nature, whose object is the emergence of a new and as yet unknown content.
>
> (CW 9i, 285)

Comment

Abandonment is regarded as a contributory causal factor to a range of mental disorders including borderline personality disorder and post-traumatic stress disorder and can make adult relationships problematic. Jung in CW 9i, para. 285 goes on to describe psychological abandonment as a condition which gives rise to an 'agonising situation of conflict' with no way out. The tension of opposites creates an irrational third thing. This is a meaningful and unknown uniting symbol which is redemptive. The AE can stimulate awareness of such tensions which sometimes surface during the context interview and, in this respect, can be therapeutic.

Aetiology (1) the cause, set of causes, or manner of causation of a disease or condition, as in 'the importance of sunlight in the aetiology of melanoma'.
(2) the investigation or attribution of the cause or reason for something, often expressed in terms of historical or mythical explanation (Bab. la 2024).

Affect 'A state of feeling characterised by marked physical innervations on the one hand and a peculiar disturbance of the ideational process on the other'.

Jung (CW 6, 681)

Affects occur usually where adaptation is weakest, and at the same time they reveal the reason for its weakness, namely a certain degree of inferiority and the existence of a lower level of personality. On this lower level with its uncontrolled or scarcely controlled emotions one . . . is not only the passive victim of his affects but also singularly incapable of moral judgment.

(CW 9ii, 15)

Jung cites Wundt:

The elements of memory images are projected, as it were, into the external object, so that particularly when the object and the reproduced elements differ substantially from one another, the finished sense impression appears as an illusion, deceiving us as to the real nature of things.

(Wundt 1874, p. 529)

Comment

Affects usually indicate that a complex has been triggered. Furthermore, affects can be considered as emotions which have temporarily taken over the personality. In popular usage, it can be said of people who are temporarily out of control, 'they are in affect'.

Analysis, Jungian A form of therapy specialising in neurosis, aimed at bringing unconscious contents to consciousness; also called analytic therapy, based on the school of thought developed by C. G. Jung called analytical (or complex) psychology.

[Analysis] is only a means for removing the stones from the path of development, and not a method . . . of putting things into the patient that were not there before. It is better to renounce any attempt to give direction, and simply try to throw into relief everything that the analysis brings to light, so that the patient can see it clearly and be able to draw suitable conclusions. Anything he has not acquired himself he will not believe in the long run, and what he takes over from authority merely keeps him infantile. He should rather be put in a position to take his own life in hand. The art of analysis lies in following the patient on all his erring ways and so gathering his strayed sheep together.

(CW 4, 643)

There is a widespread prejudice that analysis is something like a 'cure,' to which one submits for a time and is then discharged healed. That is a layman's error left over from the early days of psychoanalysis. Analytical treatment could be described as a readjustment of psychological attitude achieved with the help of the doctor . . . . (But) there is no change that is unconditionally valid over a long period of time.

(CW 8, 142)

Comment

Sharp (1936) continues his definition by explaining the difference between Freudian and Jungian approaches, whereby Jung eschewed the term 'psychoanalysis'. As both traditional psychoanalysis and Jungian analysis have evolved over time, the terms 'psychoanalyst' and 'Jungian analyst' are more commonly used interchangeably. Both deal with unconscious processes. However, there also are significant differentiations between the different schools. In view of the development of rational schools of psychotherapy, it is useful to note Jung's pragmatic position (cited by Sharp 1991, below):

Consistent support of the conscious attitude has in itself a high therapeutic value and not infrequently serves to bring about satisfactory results. It would be a dangerous prejudice to imagine that analysis of the unconscious is the one and only panacea which should therefore be employed in every case. It is rather like a surgical operation and we should only resort to the knife when other methods have failed. So long as it does not obtrude itself the unconscious is best left alone.

(CW 16, 381)

Sharp's definition is especially helpful because the term appears to be redacted from the Princeton Edition of Definitions (CW 9.1).

Association (1) A spontaneous flow of interconnected thoughts and images around a specific idea, often determined by unconscious connections. Personal associations to images in dreams, together with amplification, are an important initial step in their interpretation (Sharp 1991).

A contemporary definition, given by the American Psychological Association, embraces learning theory and behaviourism:

(2) The process by which simple perceptions and ideas are combined into totalities of varying degrees of complexity and abstractness, as, for example, connecting the relatively simple ideas of four legs, furry coat, a certain shape and size and so on into the compound concept 'cat'. The same process is held to explain one's understanding of entirely abstract ideas, such as power or liberalism. The association of ideas was a key concept for the British empiricist school of philosophers (see empiricism) and remains fundamental in learning theory and behaviorism (APA 2004).

Comment

A fundamental technique of analysis, the explorations of associations can be applied to stimulate the discovery of meaning and progression towards wholeness. The technique is also inherent in amplification and can be used to explore both the collective unconscious and social phenomena.

Autonomous   Independent of the conscious will, associated in general with the nature of the unconscious and in particular with activated **complexes** (Sharp 1991).

Comment

A differentiating feature of complexes is that they are autonomous, i.e. they can be thought of as 'split off' parts of the ego which when triggered, completely take over.

Causal   An approach to the interpretation of psychic phenomena based on cause and effect (Sharp 1991).

Comment

Causation is a central practical topic in the Word Association Experiment and particularly in the identification of complexes and their import on diagnosis of common aetiologies of mental disorders. At the same time, much has been written on the philosophy and psychology of causation from different perspectives (for example, White 1990). For example, in 1952 (around 40 years after his publications on the Word Association Test), Jung developed his approach to include 'Synchronicity: An Acausal Connecting Principle' (CW 8). Note 'Acausal'. Advanced WAT practitioners frequently report synchronicities observed during the experiment.

Complex   A group or system of related ideas or impulses that have a common emotional tone and exert a strong but usually unconscious influence on the individual's attitudes and behavior. The term, introduced by Carl Jung to denote the contents of the personal unconscious, has taken on an almost purely pathological connotation in popular usage, which does not necessarily reflect usage in psychology. Primary examples from classical psychoanalysis and its offshoots are Jung's power complex, Sigmund Freud's castration complex and Oedipus complex and Alfred Adler's inferiority complex (APA dictionary 2024).

Jung gives the following explanation:

> Every constellation of a complex postulates a disturbed state of consciousness. The unity of consciousness is disrupted and the intentions of the will are impeded or made impossible. Even memory is often noticeably affected . . . an active complex puts us momentarily under a state of duress, of compulsive thinking and acting, for which under certain conditions the only appropriate term would be the judicial concept of diminished responsibility.
> (CW 8, 200)

Sharp (1936) also cites Jung:

> The possession of complexes does not in itself signify neurosis . . . and the fact that they are painful is no proof of pathological disturbance. Suffering is not an illness; it is the normal counterpole to happiness. A complex becomes pathological only when we think we have not got it.
> (CW 16, 179)

and

> A complex can be really overcome only if it is lived out to the full. In other words, if we are to develop further we have to draw to us and drink down to the very dregs what, because of our complexes, we have held at a distance.
>
> (CW 9i, 184)

Whitaker (2019, pp. 43–55) gives a good account of the link between archetypes and complexes.

Comment

We are often faced with the challenge of recognising patterns of feeling and behaviour which defy rationality. Reflecting on our lives, we can ask; 'What came over us? What were we thinking?'

Conflict   A state of indecision, accompanied by inner tension.

> The apparently unendurable conflict is proof of the rightness of your life. A life without inner contradiction is either only half a life or else a life in the Beyond, which is destined only for angels. But God loves human beings more than the angels.
>
> (Jung 1992, p. 375)

> The self is made manifest in the opposites and in the conflict between them; it is a *coincidentia oppositorum* (coincidence of opposites). Hence the way to the self begins with conflict. (CW 12, para. 259)

Conflict is a hallmark of neurosis, but conflict is not invariably neurotic. Some degree of conflict is even desirable since without some tension between opposites the developmental process is inhibited. Conflict only becomes neurotic when it interferes with the normal functioning of consciousness.

> The stirring up of conflict is a Luciferian virtue in the true sense of the word. Conflict engenders fire, the fire of affects and emotions, and like every other fire it has two aspects, that of combustion and that of creating light.
>
> (CW 9i, 179)

When a conflict is unconscious, tension manifests as physical symptoms, particularly in the stomach, the back and the neck. Conscious conflict is experienced as moral or ethical tension. Serious conflicts, especially those involving love or duty, generally involve a disparity between the functions of thinking and feeling. If one or the other is not a conscious participant in the conflict, it needs to be introduced.

> The objection (may be) advanced that many conflicts are intrinsically insoluble. People sometimes take this view because they think only of external solutions – which at bottom are not solutions at all . . . . A real solution comes only from within, and then only because the patient has been brought to a different attitude.
>
> (CW 4, 606)

Jung's major contribution to the psychology of conflict was his belief that it had a purpose in terms of the self-regulation of the psyche. If the tension between the opposites can be held in consciousness, then something will happen internally to resolve the conflict. The solution, essentially irrational and unforeseeable, generally appears as a new attitude toward oneself and the outer situation, together with a sense of peace; energy previously locked up in indecision is released, and the progression of libido becomes possible. Jung called this the *tertium non datur* or transcendent function, because what happens transcends the opposites.

Comment

(See Abandonment.) Jung's description of conflict is well explained in CW 9i, 285.

Coniunctio Literally, 'conjunction', used in alchemy to refer to chemical combinations; psychologically, it points to the union of opposites and the birth of new possibilities.

> The coniunction is an a priori image that occupies a prominent place in the history of man's mental development. If we trace this idea back we find it has two sources in alchemy, one Christian, the other pagan. The Christian source is unmistakably the doctrine of Christ and the Church, sponsus and sponsa, where Christ takes the role of Sol and the Church that of Luna. The pagan source is on the one hand the hieros-gamos, on the other the marital union of the mystic with God.
>
> (CW 16, 355)

Other alchemical terms used by Jung with a near-equivalent psychological meaning include *unio mystica* (mystic or sacred marriage), *coincidentia oppositorum* (coincidence of opposites), *complexio oppositorum (*the opposites embodied in a single image) *unus mundus* (one world) and Philosophers' Stone (Adapted from Sharp 1991).

Comment

The idea of the union of opposites in the Western world derives from ancient and mediaeval philosophy, and is often referred to as non-duality. It is not an exclusively Christian philosophy and is found in many religions and schools of thought (for example Yab-Yum in Buddhism).

Consciousness The function or activity which maintains the relation of psychic contents to the ego; distinguished conceptually from the psyche, which encompasses both consciousness and the unconscious.

> There is no consciousness without discrimination of opposites.
>
> (CW 9i, 178)

> There are two distinct ways in which consciousness arises. The one is a moment of high emotional tension, comparable to the scene in Parsifal where the hero, at the very moment of greatest temptation, suddenly realizes the meaning of Amfortas' wound. The other is a state of contemplation, in which ideas pass before the mind like dream-images. Suddenly there is a flash of association between two apparently disconnected and widely separated ideas, and this has the effect of releasing a latent tension. Such a moment often works like a revelation. In every case it seems to be the discharge of energy-tension, whether external or internal, which produces consciousness.
>
> (CW 17, 207)

In Jung's view of the psyche, individual consciousness is a superstructure based on and arising out of the unconscious.

> Consciousness does not create itself – it wells up from unknown depths. In childhood it awakens gradually, and all through life it wakes each morning out of the depths of sleep from an unconscious condition. It is like a child that is born daily out of the primordial womb of the unconscious . . . . It is not only influenced by the unconscious but continually emerges out of it in the form of numberless spontaneous ideas and sudden flashes of thought.
> (CW 11, 935)

Counter-transference   A particular case of projection, used to describe the unconscious emotional response of the analyst to the analysand in a therapeutic relationship. (See also transference.)

> A transference is answered by a counter-transference from the analyst when it projects a content of which he is unconscious but which nevertheless exists in him. The counter-transference is then just as useful and meaningful, or as much of a hindrance, as the transference of the patient, according to whether or not it seeks to establish that better rapport which is essential for the realization of certain unconscious contents. Like the transference, the counter-transference is compulsive, a forcible tie, because it creates a 'mystical' or unconscious identity with the object.
> (CW 8, 519)

> A workable analytic relationship is predicated on the assumption that the analyst is not as neurotic as the analysand. Although a lengthy personal analysis is the major requirement in the training of analysts, this is no guarantee against projection.
> Even if the analyst has no neurosis, but only a rather more extensive area of unconsciousness than usual, this is sufficient to produce a sphere of mutual unconsciousness, i.e., a counter-transference. This phenomenon is one of the chief occupational hazards of psychotherapy. It causes psychic infections in both analyst and patient and brings the therapeutic process to a standstill. This state of unconscious identity is also the reason why an analyst can help his patient just so far as he himself has gone and not a step further.
> (CW 16, 545)

Diagnosis   The categorisation of a person's symptoms into one or more than one of an official set of disease and disorder categories based on an exploration of the symptoms a person exhibits using known patterns of symptoms as a basis for further exploration of possible symptoms (The Cambridge Dictionary of Psychology 2009).
A fuller definition is given by the American Psychological Association (2004).

> The process of identifying and determining the nature of a disease or disorder by its signs and symptoms, through the use of assessment techniques (e.g. tests and examinations) and other available evidence.
> The classification of individuals on the basis of a disease, disorder, abnormality or set of characteristics. Psychological diagnoses have been codified for professional use, notably in the DSM–IV–TR, DSM–5, and DSM-5-TR (adapted from APA 2024).

118 Glossary of terms

Comment

In the manual, 'diagnosis' connotes both signs and symptoms. The diagnostic codes used in both the ICD and DSM are based on the observation and reporting of these. While the WAT has been used as an adjunct to diagnosis and differential diagnosis of particular sign and symptoms the emphasis in this manual is the identification of common contributory causes (such as childhood abuse and neglect to mental disorders. Differential diagnosis is a method of differentiating between conditions (two or more) disorders which the process of differentiating between two or more conditions which have similar signs and/or symptoms.

Differentiation   The separation of parts from a whole, necessary for conscious access to the psychological **functions**.

So long as a function is still so fused with one or more other functions – thinking with feeling, feeling with sensation, etc. – that it is unable to operate on its own, it is in an *archaic* condition, i.e., not differentiated, not separated from the whole as a special part and existing by itself. Undifferentiated thinking is incapable of thinking apart from other functions; it is continually mixed up with sensations, feelings, intuitions, just as undifferentiated feeling is mixed up with sensations and fantasies.

(CW 6, 705)

An undifferentiated function is characterised by ambivalence (every position entails its own negative), which leads to characteristic inhibitions in its use.

Differentiation consists in the separation of the function from other functions, and in the separation of its individual parts from each other. Without differentiation direction is impossible, since the direction of a function towards a goal depends on the elimination of anything irrelevant. Fusion with the irrelevant precludes direction; only a differentiated function is *capable* of being directed (CW 6, para. 705).

DSM   *The Diagnostic and Statistical Manual of Mental Disorders* (DSM 5 TR) is a publication of the American Psychiatric Association containing lists of mental disorders, their symptoms, criteria for diagnosis and demographic information about the disorders that is used as a professional guide to diagnosis of mental disorders in the United States (see Also ICD).

A full definition is given as follows by the American Psychological Association (2015).

The fifth edition of the *Diagnostic and Statistical Manual of Mental Disorders*, prepared by the DSM–5 Task Force of the American Psychiatric Association and published in 2013. Changes from the DSM–IV–TR included use of a nonaxial approach to diagnosis with separate notations for psychosocial and contextual factors and disability; organisation of diagnoses according to the period (i.e. childhood, adolescence, adulthood, later life) during which they most frequently first manifest; clustering of disorders within chapters according to internalising factors (e.g. anxiety, depression) and externalising factors (e.g. impulsive, disruptive conduct); replacement of the 'not otherwise specified' label with 'clinician choice of other specified disorder or unspecified disorder'; replacement of the Global Assessment of Functioning Scale with the World Health Organization's Disability Assessment Schedule for further study; and consolidation of separate diagnostic areas into spectra (e.g. autism spectrum disorder).

The structure and content of the DSM–5 was coordinated with that of the 11th revision of the International Classification of Diseases (ICD-11), although DSM–5 retains diagnostic codes from both the ICD–9–Clinical Modification and ICD–10–CM. In addition, the Roman numerals used in previous DSM editions were replaced with an Arabic numeral to allow clearer labeling of future updates (e.g. DSM–5.1, DSM–5.2).

Several diagnostic changes in the DSM–5 were met with controversy. Its consolidation of Asperger's disorder into autism spectrum disorder, for example, raised concerns that those who met prior criteria for Asperger's would instead be diagnosed as having ASD, which many consider a more serious disorder, or not having either disorder, thereby losing eligibility for certain medical and educational services. Moreover, a criticism of its immediate predecessor was lodged against the DSM–5 as well – that it retained some diagnostic criteria that pathologise normal behaviors (e.g. temper tantrums, overeating) and emotions (e.g. grief, worrying).

The most recent update is the *Diagnostic and Statistical Manual of Mental Disorders, Fifth Edition, Text Revision* (DSM-5-TR), which was published in 2022 and is the first published revision of DSM-5 (APA 2015).

Emotion An involuntary reaction due to an active **complex** (see also **affect**).

On the one hand, emotion is the alchemical fire whose warmth brings everything into existence and whose heat burns all superfluities to ashes (omnes superfluitates comburit). But on the other hand, emotion is the moment when steel meets flint and a spark is struck forth, for emotion is the chief source of consciousness. There is no change from darkness to light or from inertia to movement without emotion.

(CW 9i, 179)

Empathy An introjection of the object based on the unconscious projection of subjective contents.

It is indeed true that empathy presupposes a subjective attitude of confidence, or trustfulness towards the object. It is a readiness to meet the object halfway, a subjective assimilation that brings about a good understanding between subject and object, or at least simulates it. A passive object allows itself to be assimilated subjectively, but its real qualities are in no way altered in the process.

(CW 6, 489)

In contrast to the man with an 'abstracting attitude',

The man with the empathetic attitude finds himself . . . in a world that needs his subjective feeling to give it life and soul. He animates it with himself . . . full of trust; but the other retreats mistrustfully before the daemonisation of objects and builds up a protective anti-world of abstractions.

(CW 6, 489, 492)

Comment

The epistemological views of Husserl and Edith Stein are implicit in the use of the word in this manual: From Husserl's point of view, empathy is inextricably linked with intersubjectivity.

According to Husserl, intersubjective experience plays a fundamental role in our constitution of both ourselves as objectively existing subjects, other experiencing subjects, and the objective spatial-temporal world. Transcendental phenomenology attempts to reconstruct the rational structures underlying – and making possible – these constitutive achievements.

From a first-person point of view, intersubjectivity comes in when we undergo acts of empathy. Intersubjective experience is empathic experience; it occurs in the course of our conscious attribution of intentional acts to other subjects, in the course of which we put ourselves into the other one's shoes.

(Beyer 2022)

Stein's (1917) definition is as follows:

the experience of foreign consciousness in general, irrespective of the kind of the experiencing subject or of the subject whose consciousness is experienced.

Szanto and Dermot (2020) explain that Stein's multi-dimensional account attributes to empathy the power to grasp not only another's dispositions and motivations but also the social context of a person's motivational nexus as well as her personal character (1917, p. 114).

Epistemology The term 'epistemology' comes from the Greek words 'episteme' and 'logos'. 'Episteme' can be translated as 'knowledge' or 'understanding' or 'acquaintance', while 'logos' can be translated as 'account' or 'argument' or 'reason'. Just as each of these different translations captures some facet of the meaning of these Greek terms, so too does each translation capture a different facet of epistemology itself. Although the term 'epistemology' is no more than a couple of centuries old, the field of epistemology is at least as old as any in philosophy. In different parts of its extensive history, different facets of epistemology have attracted attention. Plato's epistemology was an attempt to understand what it was to know, and how knowledge (unlike mere true opinion) is good for the knower. Locke's epistemology was an attempt to understand the operations of human understanding, Kant's epistemology was an attempt to understand the conditions of the possibility of human understanding, and Russell's epistemology was an attempt to understand how modern science could be justified by appeal to sensory experience. Much recent work in formal epistemology is an attempt to understand how our degrees of confidence are rationally constrained by our evidence, and much recent work in feminist epistemology is an attempt to understand the ways in which interests affect our evidence and affect our rational constraints more generally. In all these cases, epistemology seeks to understand one or another kind of *cognitive success* (or, correspondingly, cognitive *failure*).

(Steup, 2024)

Comment

Also, an introductory exploration of an epistemology for analytical psychology is given by Ferreira Vieira (2022).

Fractal A geometric shape that can be divided into parts that each resembles the pattern of the whole shape. Thus, a fractal is a shape possessing the quality of self-similarity (APA 2024).

A fractal is a never-ending pattern. Fractals are infinitely complex patterns that are self-similar across different scales. They are created by repeating a simple process over and over in an ongoing feedback loop. Driven by recursion, fractals are images of dynamic systems – the pictures of chaos. Geometrically, they exist in between our familiar dimensions. Fractal patterns are extremely familiar, since nature is full of fractals. For instance: Trees, rivers, coastlines, mountains, clouds, seashells, hurricanes, etc. Abstract fractals – such as the Mandelbrot Set – can be generated by a computer calculating a simple equation over and over (The Fractal Foundation 2024).

GAF The Global Assessment of Functioning, or GAF, scale is used to rate how serious a mental illness may be. It measures how much a person's symptoms affect their day-to-day life on a scale of 0 to 100.

It's designed to help mental health providers understand how well the person can do everyday activities. The score can help figure out what level of care someone may need and how well certain treatments might work.

The GAF is based on a scale that was first used in 1962. It's been updated over time. In 2013, the manual that psychiatrists in the U.S. use to define and classify mental disorders dropped it in favor of a scale designed by the World Health Organization. But government agencies and insurance companies, as well as others, still use it and aren't expected to replace it anytime soon (Smith 2004; see Appendix 3).

Feeling The psychological **function** that evaluates or judges what something or someone is worth (compare **thinking**).

A feeling is as indisputable a reality as the existence of an idea (CW 16, 531).

The feeling function is the basis for 'fight or flight' decisions. As a subjective process, it may be quite independent of external stimuli. In Jung's view it is a rational function, like thinking, in that it is decisively influenced not by perception (as are the functions of sensation and intuition) but by reflection. A person whose overall attitude is oriented by the feeling function is called a feeling type.

In everyday usage, feeling is often confused with emotion. The latter, more appropriately called affect, is the result of an activated complex. Feeling not contaminated by affect can be quite cold.

Feeling is distinguished from affect by the fact that it produces no perceptible physical innervations, i.e. neither more nor less than an ordinary thinking process (CW 6, 725).

Individual Unique and unlike anyone else, distinguished from what is **collective** (see also **individuality**).

A distinction must be made between individuality and the individual. The individual is determined on the one hand by the principle of uniqueness and distinctiveness, and on the other by the society to which he belongs. He is an indispensable link in the social structure.

(CW 7, 519)

The individual is precisely that which can never be merged with the collective and is never identical with it (CW 7, 485).

The larger a community is, and the more the sum total of collective factors peculiar to every large community rests on conservative prejudices detrimental to individuality, the more will the individual be morally and spiritually crushed, and, as a result, the one source of moral and spiritual progress for society is choked up.

(CW 7, 240)

The individual standpoint is not antagonistic to collective norms, only differently oriented.
    The individual way can never be directly opposed to the collective norm, because the opposite of the collective norm could only be another, but contrary, norm. But the individual way can, by definition, never be a norm.

(CW 6, 761)

Jung believed that the survival of the individual within a group depended not only on psychological self-understanding, but also on the personal experience of a higher truth.

> The individual will never find the real justification for his existence and his own spiritual and moral autonomy anywhere except in an extramundane principle capable of relativizing the overpowering influence of external factors.... For this he needs the evidence of inner, transcendent experience which alone can protect him from the otherwise inevitable submersion in the mass.
>
> (CW 10, 511)

> Resistance to the organized mass can be effected only by the man who is as well organized in his individuality as the mass itself.
>
> (540) (Sharp 1991)

Individuation A process of psychological differentiation, having for its goal the development of the individual personality.

> The aim of individuation is nothing less than to divest the self of the false wrappings of the persona on the one hand, and of the suggestive power of primordial images on the other.
>
> (CW 7, 269)

Individuation is a process informed by the archetypal ideal of wholeness, which in turn depends on a vital relationship between ego and unconscious. The aim is not to overcome one's personal psychology, to become perfect, but to become familiar with it. Thus individuation involves an increasing awareness of one's unique psychological reality, including personal strengths and limitations, and at the same time a deeper appreciation of humanity in general.

> As the individual is not just a single, separate being, but by his very existence presupposes a collective relationship, it follows that the process of individuation must lead to more intense and broader collective relationships and not to isolation.
>
> (CW 6, 758)

> Individuation does not shut one out from the world, but gathers the world to itself.
>
> (CW 8, 432)

> Individuation has two principle aspects: In the first place it is an internal and subjective process of integration, and in the second it is an equally indispensable process of objective relationship. Neither can exist without the other, although sometimes the one and sometimes the other predominates.
>
> (CW 16, 448)

Individuation and a life lived by collective values are nevertheless two divergent destinies. In Jung's view they are related to one another by guilt. Whoever embarks on the personal path becomes to some extent estranged from collective values but does not thereby lose those aspects of the psyche which are inherently collective. To atone for this 'desertion,' the individual is obliged to create something of worth for the benefit of society.

> Individuation cuts one off from personal conformity and hence from collectivity. That is the guilt which the individuant leaves behind him for the world, that is the guilt he must

endeavor to redeem. He must offer a ransom in place of himself, that is, he must bring forth values which are an equivalent substitute for his absence in the collective personal sphere. Without this production of values, final individuation is immoral and-more than that-suicidal . . . . The individuant has no a priori claim to any kind of esteem. He has to be content with whatever esteem flows to him from outside by virtue of the values he creates. Not only has society a right, it also has a duty to condemn the individuant if he fails to create equivalent values.

(CW 18, 1095f)

Individuation differs from individualism in that the former deviates from collective norms but retains respect for them, while the latter eschews them entirely.

A real conflict with the collective norm arises only when an individual way is raised to a norm, which is the actual aim of extreme individualism. Naturally this aim is pathological and inimical to life. It has, accordingly, nothing to do with individuation, which, though it may strike out on an individual bypath, precisely on that account needs the norm for its orientation to society and for the vitally necessary relationship of the individual to society. Individuation, therefore, leads to a natural esteem for the collective norm.

(CW 6, 761)

The process of individuation, consciously pursued, leads to the realisation of the self as a psychic reality greater than the ego. Thus individuation is essentially different from the process of simply becoming conscious.

The goal of the individuation process is the synthesis of the self.

(CW 9i, 278)

Again and again I note that the individuation process is confused with the coming of the ego into consciousness and that the ego is in consequence identified with the self, which naturally produces a hopeless conceptual muddle. Individuation is then nothing but ego-centredness and autoeroticism. But the self comprises infinitely more than a mere ego, as the symbolism has shown from of old. It is as much one's self, and all other selves, as the ego.

(CW 8, 432)

In Jung's view, no one is ever completely individuated. While the goal is wholeness and a healthy working relationship with the self, the true value of individuation lies in what happens along the way.

The goal is important only as an idea; the essential thing is the opus which leads to the goal: That is the goal of a lifetime.

(CW 16, 400)

Limbic system A group of structures in the brain that governs emotions, motivation, olfaction (sense of smell) and behaviour. The limbic system is also involved in the formation of long-term memory. The structures of the limbic system are found deep inside the brain, immediately below the temporal lobes and buried under the cerebral cortex, just above the brainstem. The limbic system consists of several interconnected components, including the thalamus, hypothalamus, basal ganglia, cingulate gyrus, hippocampus and amygdala (Raikar, 2024).

124 *Glossary of terms*

Meaning   The quality ascribed to something that gives it value.
An eloquent account of the meaning of meaning is given by Samuel et al. (1986).

> The question of meaning was central to Jung and to all that he undertook as person, doctor, therapist; as someone who wrestled constantly with problems of good and evil, light and dark, life and death; as a scientist and as a man of deeply religious temperament. He concluded that the locus of meaning is in psyche and psyche alone is capable of discerning the meaning of what is experienced. This underlines the crucial function of reflection in psychological life and emphasises that consciousness is not confined to the intellect. Meaning was fundamental to Jung's concept of the aetiology of neurosis since the recognition of meaning appears to have a curative power. 'A psychoneurosis must be understood, ultimately, as the suffering of a soul which has not discovered its meaning' (CW 11, para. 497). At the same time, however, though intent upon The discovery of meaning, Jung remained open to the possibility of life's meaninglessness. He perceived meaning to be paradoxical in nature and conceived it as an archetype. Consistent with this approach, Jung considered each answer to the question of meaning to be a human interpretation, a conjecture, a confession or a belief. Whatever may be the answer given to the ultimate question of life's meaning, he maintained that the answer is created by a person's own consciousness and its formulation is, therefore, a myth, since man is not capable of uncovering absolute truth. Without a means of establishing objective meaning, we rely upon subjective verification as our ultimate measure and it is upon this that analyst and patient must also rely psychotherapeutically. But the discovery of meaning is at the same time an experience attended by numinosity and accompanied by a sense of the awesome, the mysterious and the terrifying which are always connected to an experience of the divine, in whatever lowly, unacceptable, obscure or despised form it may appear. Jung's own myth of meaning seems to be inextricably linked to consciousness. Meaning is revealed by consciousness and, therefore consciousness has a spiritual as well as a cognitive function. 'Without the reflecting consciousness of man the world is a gigantic, meaningless machine, for as far as we know man is the only creature that can discover Meaning', he wrote in a letter in 1959. After intensive work upon synchronicity he concluded that, in addition to cause and effect, there is another factor in nature which is shown by the arrangement of events; this appears to us in the guise of meaning. But when asked who or what creates that meaning, his answer was not god but rather a person's own god-image.

The second half of their explanation makes critical background reading for AE practitioners, insofar as it expresses the *leitmotif* of his work, i.e. the relationship between the union of opposites (objective and subjective) and their potential union in the domain of psychotherapy.

Jaffe, Jung's secretary, has drawn together an account of his encounters with meaning and the

> conclusions on the subject that he drew from his life and work (19784). Jung, following his teacher Janet in France, and along with Forel in Switzerland and Freud in Austria, pioneered in establishing public awareness that the root cause of neurosis is psychogenic in nature. Until world war one the prevailing assumption, both medical and psychiatric, was that this and all so-called mental illnesses were diseases of the brain. From the outset of his career, Jung disagreed with the emphasis upon anatomical researches into mental illness and turned his attention instead to the content of psychosis (along with neurosis). He adopted a standpoint which affirmed the role of psychogenesis in

relation to schizophrenia and, by analysis of the delusions and hallucinations which accompanied it, established the fact that these were significant psychic products. Thus, he could go on to concern himself further with the psychology of the illness and to adopt a psychotherapeutic approach to its treatment. It is important to note, however, that although bringing relief to the patient, this approach was not considered sufficient as a cure. Jung's life-long emphasis was upon the interaction between illness and its psychological manifestations.

Neurotransmitters Neurotransmitters are often referred to as the body's chemical messengers. They are the molecules used by the nervous system to transmit messages between neurons or from neurons to muscles.

Communication between two neurons happens in the synaptic cleft (the small gap between the synapses of neurons). Here, electrical signals that have travelled along the axon are briefly converted into chemical ones through the release of neurotransmitters, causing a specific response in the receiving neuron.

A neurotransmitter influences a neuron in one of three ways: Excitatory, inhibitory or modulatory (Queensland Brain Institute 2024).

Opposites Psychologically, the ego and the unconscious (see also **compensation, conflict, progression** and **transcendent function**).

> There is no consciousness without discrimination of opposites.
>
> (CW 9i, 178)

> There is no form of human tragedy that does not in some measure proceed from (the) conflict between the ego and the unconscious.
>
> (CW 8, 706)

> Whatever attitude exists in the conscious mind, and whichever psychological function is dominant, the opposite is in the unconscious. This situation seldom precipitates a crisis in the first half of life. But for older people who reach an impasse, characterized by a one-sided conscious attitude and the blockage of energy, it is necessary to bring to light psychic contents that have been repressed.
>
> The repressed content must be made conscious so as to produce a tension of opposites, without which no forward movement is possible. The conscious mind is on top, the shadow underneath, and just as high always longs for low and hot for cold, so all consciousness, perhaps without being aware of it, seeks its unconscious opposite, lacking which it is doomed to stagnation, congestion, and ossification. Life is born only of the spark of opposites.
>
> (CW 7, 78)

This in turn activates the process of compensation, which leads to an irrational 'third,' the transcendent function.

> Out of (the) collision of opposites the unconscious psyche always creates a third thing of an irrational nature, which the conscious mind neither expects nor understands. It presents itself in a form that is neither a straight 'yes' nor a straight 'no'.
>
> (CW 9i, 285)

Jung explained the potential renewal of the personality in terms of the principle of entropy in physics, according to which transformations of energy in a relatively closed system take place and are only possible as a result of differences in intensity.

> Psychologically, we can see this process at work in the development of a lasting and relatively unchanging attitude. After violent oscillations at the beginning the opposites equalize one another, and gradually a new attitude develops, the final stability of which is the greater in proportion to the magnitude of the initial differences. The greater the tension between the pairs of opposites, the greater will be the energy that comes from them ... (and) the less chance is there of subsequent disturbances which might arise from friction with material not previously constellated.
>
> ('On Psychic Energy,' CW 8, 49)

> The united personality will never quite lose the painful sense of innate discord. Complete redemption from the sufferings of this world is and must remain an illusion. Christ's earthly life likewise ended, not in complacent bliss, but on the cross.
>
> (CW 16, 400)

Jung further believed that anyone who attempts to deal with the problem of the opposites on a personal level is making a significant contribution toward world peace (adapted from Sharp 1991).

Projective technique Any assessment procedure that consists of a series of relatively ambiguous stimuli designed to elicit unique, sometimes highly idiosyncratic responses that reflect the personality, cognitive style, and other psychological characteristics of the respondent. Examples of this type of procedure are the Rorschach Inkblot Test and the Thematic Apperception Test as well as sentence-completion, word-association and drawing tests. The use of projective techniques has generated considerable discussion among researchers, with opinions ranging from the expressed belief that personality assessment is incomplete without data from at least one or more of these procedures to the assertion that such techniques lack important psychometric features such as reliability and validity. Also called projective method (APA 2024).

Psychological tests Also known as psychometric tests, these are standardised instruments that are used to measure behavior or mental attributes. These attributes may include attitudes, emotional functioning, intelligence and cognitive abilities, aptitude, values, interests, personality characteristics and more.

Psychological tests may also be used to evaluate mental health, such as psychological functioning or signs of psychological or neurological disorders (APA 2004).

Reliability The trustworthiness or consistency of a measure, that is, the degree to which a test or other measurement instrument is free of random error, yielding the same results across multiple applications to the same sample. See alternate-forms reliability; internal consistency; reliability coefficient; retest reliability (APA 2024).

Signs and symptoms Simply put, 'Signs are observable indications of a disorder, whereas symptoms are self-report of the physical or psychological effects of a disorder' (Kraft & Keeley 2015). It can be said that symptoms are what the patient experiences and signs are what the practitioner observes. A practical reference is the Mental Status Examination. While this is beyond the scope of WAE training, it is a good example of part of the psychiatric assessment process (Sadock & Sadok 2007, pp. 232–237).

Splitting   A term used to describe the **dissociation** of the personality, marked by attitudes and behavior patterns determined by **complexes**.

> Although this peculiarity is most clearly observable in psychopathology, fundamentally it is a normal phenomenon, which can be recognized with the greatest ease in the projections made by the primitive psyche. The tendency to split means that parts of the psyche detach themselves from consciousness to such an extent that they not only appear foreign but lead an autonomous life of their own. It need not be a question of hysterical multiple personality, or schizophrenic alterations of personality, but merely of so-called 'complexes' that come entirely within the scope of the normal.
>
> (CW 8, 253)

Subjective level   The approach to dreams and other images in which the persons or situations pictured are seen as symbolic representations of factors belonging entirely to the subject's own psyche.

> Interpretation of an unconscious product on the subjective level reveals the presence of subjective judgements and tendencies of which the object is made the vehicle. When, therefore, an object-imago appears in an unconscious product, it is not on that account the image of a real object; it is far more likely that we are dealing with a subjective functional complex. Interpretation on the subjective level allows us to take a broader psychological view not only of dreams but also of literary works, in which the individual figures then appear as representatives of relatively autonomous functional complexes in the psyche of the author.
>
> (CW 6, 813)

> In the analytic process, the main task after the reductive interpretation of images thrown up by the unconscious is to understand what they say about oneself.
>   To establish a really mature attitude, he has to see the *subjective* value of all these images which seem to create trouble for him. He has to assimilate them into his own psychology; he has to find out in what way they are part of himself; how he attributes for instance a positive value to an *object*, when as a matter of fact it is he who could and should develop this value. And in the same way, when he projects negative qualities and therefore hates and loathes the object, he has to discover that he is projecting his own inferior side, his shadow, as it were, because he prefers to have an optimistic and one-sided image of himself.
>
> (CW 6, para. 813) (Adapted from Sharp 1991)

Test   Any of a class of statistical tests based on the fact that the test statistic follows the *t* distribution when the null hypothesis is true. Most t tests deal with hypotheses about the mean of a population or about differences between means of different populations, where those populations show normal distributions and the variances are unknown and need to be estimated. The test can be used with independent groups (e.g. test scores of those who were given training vs. a control group without training) or dependent groups (e.g. test scores before vs. after training).

Transference   A particular case of **projection**, used to describe the unconscious, emotional bond that arises in the analysand toward the analyst (see also **counter-transference**).

> Unconscious contents are invariably projected at first upon concrete persons and situations. Many projections can ultimately be integrated back into the individual once

he has recognised their subjective origin; others resist integration, and although they may be detached from their original objects, they thereupon transfer themselves to the doctor. Among these contents the relation to the parent of opposite sex plays an important part, i.e. the relation of son to mother, daughter to father, and also that of brother to sister.

(CW 16, 357)

Once the projections are recognized as such, the particular form of rapport known as the transference is at an end, and the problem of individual relationship begins.

(CW 16, 287)

A transference may be either positive or negative; the former is marked by feelings of affection and respect, the latter by hostility and resistance.

For one type of person (called the infantile-rebel) a positive transference is, to begin with, an important achievement with a healing significance; for the other (the infantile-obedient) it is a dangerous backsliding, a convenient way of evading life's duties. For the first a negative transference denotes increased insubordination, hence a backsliding and an evasion of life's duties, for the second it is a step forward with a healing significance.

(CW 4, 659)

Jung did not regard the transference merely as a projection of infantile-erotic fantasies. Though these may be present at the beginning of analysis, they can be dissolved through the reductive method. Then the purpose of the transference becomes the main issue and guide.

An exclusively sexual interpretation of dreams and fantasies is a shocking violation of the patient's psychological material: Infantile-sexual fantasy is by no means the whole story, since the material also contains a creative element, the purpose of which is to shape a way out of the neurosis.

(CW 16, 277)

Although Jung made contradictory statements about the therapeutic importance of the transference – for instance:

The transference phenomenon is an inevitable feature of every thorough analysis, for it is imperative that the doctor should get into the closest possible touch with the patient's line of psychological development.

(CW 16, 283)

We do not work with the 'transference to the analyst,' but *against it and in spite of it*.

(CW 4, 601)

A transference is always a hindrance; it is never an advantage.

(CW 18, 349)

Medical treatment of the transference gives the patient a priceless opportunity to withdraw his projections, to make good his losses, and to integrate his personality.

(CW 16, 420)

He did not doubt its significance when it was present.

> The suitably trained analyst mediates the transcendent function for the patient, i.e., helps him to bring conscious and unconscious together and so arrive at a new attitude . . . . The patient clings by means of the transference to the person who seems to promise him a renewal of attitude; through it he seeks this change, which is vital to him, even though he may not be conscious of doing so. For the patient, therefore, the analyst has the character of an indispensable figure absolutely necessary for life.
>
> (CW 8, 146)

Whatever is unconscious in the analysand and needed for healthy functioning is projected onto the analyst. This includes archetypal images of wholeness, with the result that the analyst takes on the stature of a mana-personality. The analysand's task is then to understand such images on the subjective level, a primary aim being to constellate the patient's own inner analyst.

> Empathy is an important purposive element in the transference. By means of empathy the analysand attempts to emulate the presumably healthier attitude of the analyst, and thereby to attain a better level of adaptation. The patient is bound to the analyst by ties of affection or resistance and cannot help following and imitating his psychic attitude. By this means he feels his way along (empathy). And with the best will in the world and for all his technical skill the analyst cannot prevent it, for empathy works surely and instinctively in spite of conscious judgment, be it never so strong.
>
> (CW 4, 661)

Jung believed that analyzing the transference was extremely important in order to return projected contents necessary for the individuation of the analysand. But he pointed out that even after projections have been withdrawn there remains a strong connection between the two parties. This is because of an instinctive factor that has few outlets in modern society: Kinship libido.

> Everyone is now a stranger among strangers. Kinship libido-which could still engender a satisfying feeling of belonging together, as for instance in the early Christian communities-has long been deprived of its object. But, being an instinct, it is not to be satisfied by any mere substitute such as a creed, party, nation, or state. It wants the human connection. That is the core of the whole transference phenomenon, and it is impossible to argue it away, because relationship to the self is at once relationship to our fellow man, and no one can be related to the latter until he is related to himself.
>
> (CW 16, 445)

Typology A means of describing and understanding attitudes and behaviour patterns, devised by Jung. The two major references are 'A theory of psychological types' (CW 6, paras. 883–949) and 'Psychological typology' (CW 6, paras. 960–987).

> It is not the purpose of a psychological typology to classify human beings into categories – this in itself would be pretty pointless. Its purpose is rather to provide a critical psychology which will make a methodological investigation of the empirical material possible. First and foremost, it is a critical tool for the research worker, who needs definite points of view and guidelines if he is to reduce the chaotic profusion of individual experiences to any kind of order . . . . Secondly, a typology is a great help in understanding the wide variations that occur among individuals, and it also furnishes a clue to the fundamental differences in the psychological theories now current. Last but not least, it is an essential means for determining the 'personal

equation' of the practising psychologist, who, armed with an exact knowledge of his differentiated and inferior functions, can avoid many serious blunders in dealing with his patients.

(CW 6, 986)

Jung differentiated eight typological groups: Two personality attitudes (introversion and extraversion) and four functions (thinking, sensation, intuition and feeling), each of which may operate in an introverted or extroverted way.

I would not for anything dispense with this compass on my psychological voyages of discovery . . . I value the type theory for the objective reason that it provides a system of comparison and orientation which makes possible something that has long been lacking, a critical psychology.

(CW 6, 959)

A neuroscience perspective is offered by (Escamilla 2021, pp. 49–51).

Comment

Jung advised the observation of types in the Association Experiment (Chapter 7 of this volume).

Tertium Non Datur The principle that one (and one only) of two contradictory propositions must be true.

As a rule it occurs when the analysis has constellated the opposites so powerfully that a union or synthesis of the personality becomes an imperative necessity . . . [This situation] requires a real solution and necessitates a third thing in which the opposites can unite. Here the logic of the intellect usually fails, for in a logical antithesis there is no third. The 'solvent' can only be of an irrational nature. In nature the resolution of opposites is always an energic process: She acts *symbolically* in the truest sense of the word, doing something that expresses both sides, just as a waterfall visibly mediates between above and below.

(CW 14, 705)

Comment

It can be considered a phenomenon of binary logic which creates a necessary but temporary impasse in the necessary differentiation stage of individuation as described by Jung.

Unconsciousness A state of psychic functioning marked by lack of control over the instincts and **identification** with **complexes**.
Unconsciousness is the primal sin, evil itself, for the Logos (CW 9i, 178).

An extreme state of unconsciousness is characterized by the predominance of compulsive instinctual processes, the result of which is either uncontrolled inhibition or a lack of inhibition throughout. The happenings within the psyche are then contradictory and proceed in terms of alternating, non-logical antitheses. In such a case the level of consciousness is essentially that of a dream-state. A high degree of consciousness, on the other hand, is characterized by a heightened awareness, a preponderance of will, directed, rational behaviour, and an almost total absence of instinctual determinants. The unconscious is then found to be at a definitely animal level. The first state is lacking in intellectual and ethical achievement, the second lacks naturalness.

(CW 8, 249)

The greatest danger about unconsciousness is proneness to suggestion. The effect of suggestion is due to the release of an unconscious dynamic, and the more unconscious this is, the more effective it will be. Hence the ever-widening split between conscious and unconscious increases the danger of psychic infection and mass psychosis.

(CW 9ii, 390)

Validity   the degree to which empirical evidence and theoretical rationales support the adequacy and appropriateness of conclusions drawn from some form of assessment. Validity has multiple forms, depending on the research question and on the particular type of inference being made. For example, the three major types of test validity are criterion validity, based on correlation with an accepted standard; construct validity, based on the conceptual variable underlying a test; and content validity, based on the subject matter of a test. Other forms of validity prominent in the social sciences include ecological validity, external validity, internal validity and statistical conclusion validity (APA 2024).

Validity criterion   An external concept or standard of comparison that is used to define the attribute an instrument is purported to measure and that is applied in estimating how well the measurement instrument actually fulfills its intended purpose (APA 2024).

Word Association Experiment   A test devised by Jung to show the reality and autonomy of unconscious complexes.

Our conscious intentions and actions are often frustrated by unconscious processes whose very existence is a continual surprise to us. We make slips of the tongue and slips in writing and unconsciously do things that betray our most closely guarded secrets – which are sometimes unknown even to ourselves . . . . These phenomena can . . . be demonstrated experimentally by the association tests, which are very useful for finding out things that people cannot or will not speak about.

(CW 8, 296)

The Association Experiment consists of a list of one hundred words, to which one is asked to give an immediate association. The person conducting the experiment measures the delay in response with a stop watch. This is repeated a second time, noting any different responses. Finally the subject is asked for comments on those words to which there were a longer-than-average response time, a merely mechanical response, or a different association on the second run-through; all these are marked by the questioner as 'complex indicators' and then discussed with the subject.

The result is a 'map' of the personal complexes, valuable both for self-understanding and in recognizing disruptive factors that commonly bedevil relationships.

(Sharp, 1991)

What happens in the association test also happens in every discussion between two people . . . . The discussion loses its objective character and its real purpose, since the constellated complexes frustrate the intentions of the speakers and may even put answers into their mouths which they can no longer remember afterwards.

(A Review of the Complex Theory,' CW 8, 199)

132 *Glossary of terms*

Word Association Test is a test in which the participant responds to a stimulus word with the first word that comes to mind. The technique was invented by Francis Galton in 1879 for use in exploring individual differences, and Emil Kraepelin was the first to apply it to the study of abnormality. Carl Jung and other psychoanalysts later adapted it for use as a projective technique (APA 2024).

Shamdashani (2003, p. 30) states, 'The general attitude towards Jung's work in academic psychology has been that his early experimental studies on word associations were 'scientific' and that his work on psychological types presents some hypotheses which are amenable to experimentation'.

It is also defined as:

Any of numerous measures of personality, pathology, and mental deficiency in which a subject is asked to respond as quickly as possible with the first word that comes to mind, and reaction time as well as the content of the response are analyzed. This measure was first devised by Carl Jung in order to investigate the mental functioning of schizophrenics.

Reliability and validity for this measure are largely lacking, although many clinicians claim it gives considerable insight into clients.

(The Cambridge Dictionary of Psychology 2009)

Comment

The earlier definitions of the Word Association Test are used in the manual. Jung also calls the Word Association Experiment, the Word Association Test. Reliability and validity of Jung's Word Association Test have been empirically validated (see Chapter 11).

References

American Psychological Association (APA). 2015, *APA Dictionary of Psychology*. Visited March 12, 2024. <https://dictionary.apa.org/>.
Bab.la. Visited March 14, 2024. <https://en.bab.la/dictionary/english/aetiology>.
Beyer, C 2022, 'Edmund Husserl', In N Edward & U Nodelman (Eds.), <https://plato.stanford.edu/archives/win2022/entries/husserl/>.
The Cambridge Dictionary of Psychology 2009, D Matsumoto (Ed.), Cambridge University Press, Cambridge.
Escamilla, M 2021, 'Neuroscience and Jung', In N O'Brien & J O'Brien (Eds.), *The Professional Practice of Jungian Coaching*, Routledge, Hove.
The Fractal Foundation. Visited March 11, 2024. <https://fractalfoundation.org/resources/what-are-fractals/>.
Jaffe, A 1984, *The Myth of Meaning in the Work of C. G. Jung*, Deimon Verlag, Einsiedeln.
Jung, CG 1992, *C G Jung Letters, vol. 1*, trans. G Adler and A Jaffe, Princeton University Press, Princeton.
Jung, CG 2000, *The Collected Works of C. G. Jung* (CW), eds. H Read, M Fordham, G Adler and W McGuire, trans. RFC Hull, CWs 3–18, Princeton University Press, Princeton.
Kraft, N, Keeley, J 2015, 'Sign versus symptom', In RL Cautin & SO Lilienfeld (Eds.), *The Encyclopedia of Clinical Psychology*. Wiley-Blackwell. <doi: 10.1002/9781118625392.wbecp145>.
Raikar, SP 2024. 'limbic system'. *Encyclopedia Britannica*, 26 Sep. 2024, https://www.britannica.com/science/limbic-system. Accessed 15 October 2024.
Ruiz, P, Shah, A, Kaplan, HI, & Sadock, BJ 2022. Kaplan & Sadock's synopsis of psychiatry. R. J. Boland & M. L. Verduin, (Eds.), Twelfth edition. Wolters Kluwer. <https://emergency.lwwhealthlibrary.com/book.aspx?bookid=3071>.
Queensland Brain Institute, University of Queensland. Visited March 11, 2024. <https://research.uq.edu.au/>.
Sadock, M, Sadock, V 2007, *Synopsis of Psychiatry* (10th ed.), Lippincott Williams & Wilkins, Philadelphia.
Sharp, D 1991, *Jung Lexicon: A Primer of Terms and Concepts*, Inner City Books, New York.

Smith, M 2004, 'What is the Global Assessment of Functioning (GAF) scale?', *WebMD*. Visited March 11, 2024. <www.google.com/search?q=GAF+The+Global+Assessment+of+Functioning>.

Stein, E [1917] 1964, 'On the problem of empathy', *Springer Science Business Media*. Visited March 12, 2024, <https://stmaryscathedral.ca/wp-content/uploads/2022/07/On-the-Problem-of-Empathy-Edith-Stein-auth-z-liborg.pdf>.

Steup, M, Ram, N, 2024. 'Epistemology', *The Stanford Encyclopedia of Philosophy (Spring 2024 Edition)*, Edward N. Zalta & Uri Nodelman (eds.)

Szanto, T, Dermot, M 2020, 'Edith Stein', *The Stanford Encyclopedia of Philosophy*. Visited March 12, 2024. <https://plato.stanford.edu/archives/spr2020/entries/stein/>.

Vanden Bos, G (ed.) 2007, *APA Dictionary of Psychology*. Visited March 12, 2024. <https://dictionary.apa.org/>.

Vieira, T 2022, 'Introduction to an epistemology for analytical psychology in a civilization in transition', *Journal of Analytical Psychology*, vol. 67, no. 2, pp. 711–727. <doi: 10.1111/1468-5922.12812>.

Whitaker, B 2019, 'The word association experiment', in J O'Brien & N O'Brien (Eds.), *Introduction to Corporate Analytical Psychology*, Dosije studio, Belgrade.

White, P 1990, 'Ideas about causation in philosophy and psychology', *Psychological Bulletin*, vol. 108, no. 1. <doi: 10.1037/0033-2909.108.1.3>.

Wundt, W 1874, *Grundzüge de physiologischen Psychologie*, W. Engelman, Leipzig.

Appendix 1

Note on further research: Recursive analysis

This section is included for those interested in further research and advanced experimental practice. It is not required for the examination.

Recursive analysis

In accordance with the recursive nature of analytic enquiry, described further depth of understanding can by a partial repetition of Jung's procedure, only this time applied to the context interview itself.

Stimulus words which evoked significant emotional charges in part 1 of the experiment were noted and presented at the complex interview. During the context interview, the search for meaning and the patient's memory network was stimulated, with the patient often reflecting upon their own responses and producing new words, linkages and contextual meanings, with greater emphasis on the patient's own frame of reference.

A following exercise, presently based purely on word association and undertaken offline (at the experimenter's desk) appears to yield access to deeper layers of the associative memory network and to yield improved therapeutic benefit (although precisely how much has yet to be determined).

The stimulus words selected for the context interview are listed again in descending order of charge (high to low number of complex indicators). It can be helpful for future experimentation to give a classification code and valency weighting to each item.

Next, an examination of the transcript of the context interview will reveal a deeper layer of words, phrases and sentences which form both associative memory networks and derivative commentary on the patient's experience of the experiment. The deeper layer of words can reveal a new category of repeated and/or emotionally charged words which are meaningful to the client and which are traceable back to the stimulus word. These words can also be meaningfully connected across the different chains of association.

As should now be clear, this exploration could take a long time! It is possible to use software to explore the connections between specific words and other words and phrases, and this could be an interesting research exercise for those interested in associative memory networks. For the time being it is quite sufficient for the experimenter to examine the transcript and make a few obvious connections to inform the interpretation hypothesis, but a full method can be applied based on the following example.

Re-examination of the context interview transcript

Stimulus word: Free

Free space. No barriers, constraints, simply peace within, peaceful, blue, infinite, big, not without rules, but without norms. Simply that it is peace and endlessly big and that you draw happiness and energy from it.

A house on the island comes to mind where we used to go all the time. When I look – I see a lighthouse to the right and a e space behind. I always wondered what was there . . . I feel peace when I see that broadness. We used to go there between 7 and 22 years of age both summer and winter.

I don't think I am very free. First I do not have a freedom to do all the time what I want. Before I usually did what I thought I had or should do. It is better now but I was rarely me. Freedom is when you are who you are and somebody either loves you or not. To be who you are is freedom for me.

Stimulus word: Kiss

I constantly have that sound 'sljap'. I hated when my aunts and alike 'lick' me and hug me . . . oh how cute she is, oh how sweet and then they would pinch my cheek . . . uh it annoyed me enormously! I got fewest kisses from my father, everybody else was 'licking' me and I hated it. As a child I did not like to speak and they made me speak all the time.

There was a teacher in my school who constantly forced me to speak (I was 4 years old). Even today I am quiet in a company of people I do not know well. I remember that she was pulling my hair so much, I still wouldn't speak, at the end when she stopped I told her 'You ass!' and then she started hugging me and kissing me so that I felt sick. Once I got beaten by my father when I was 8–9 years old with his belt and an hour after he came to me crying and apologising, he thought I ran away from home and there was a mad client who was threatening him . . . he got afraid that something happened to me. When he approached to me to kiss me I hated it and I still hear that 'sljap' sound . . . (she was quiet for a while, as if thinking of something else) It has nothing to do with romantic male-female kisses; I like those kinds of kisses.

Stimulus word: Naked

No constraints, it associates me of that freedom, nothing is constraining me. I never wanted to be naked, I remember being 3 years old on the beach, feeling very shy. I was embarrassed, thinking I was ugly, that I had some fault that people are looking at me . . . I remember my mother entering the kitchen in her night gown and my father shouting at her to 'cover herself' and that she should be ashamed to show herself Alike that in front of me (7–8 years of age). Each August the 10th (my birthday) my mother took me to the photographer to take a picture of me. She dressed me in the clothes I disliked and when I was 14 years of age I said I did not want to do it anymore. It was like doing a sentence, I cried every time. It was important to my mother that I looked as a doll. The only thing I liked was my knitted socks. They always went to people (and took me with them) without children. She liked combing my hair and making different coiffures. I was frustrated I couldn't be me. My only freedom was when I was with an animal and did whatever I wanted with it. My mother never bought anything new for me, I did not have my own coat till I was 16, I was inheriting other people's clothes. Nowadays I buy clothes uncontrollably and never have any. First thing she bought for me was a tweed jacket when I was 15. It was important to my father that I was dressed like a proper girl. My parents were never naked in front of me. I remember my potty. I had problems defecating (3–4 years of age). They made me sit on the potty for hours. Till 3 years ago, I was not able to empty my bowels regularly.

Stimulus word: Boss

I hate rules (norms), especially if I do not understand them. I did not like them as a child; I do not like them now. I hate when somebody tells me you have to. It took me many years to understand that I don't have to; it is I want or do not want to, not I have to. I always had rules imposed on me (you must not sit at the table with grown up, you have to go to the shops, you have to be quiet, you must not talk back . . ., while you are under my roof it has to be like I want . . .). Where there are too many rules imposed – anarchy is created. In my work I always tried to develop and go up the ladder very quickly, to be one step above from others, so that those imposed rules are lesser, so that I could be more creative, make a decision not only obey.

Stimulus word: Family

It was always like in a beehive. Always too many people, my mother was 'tied' to her sister and I am absolutely positive that she loved them more than me. Aunt and uncle were teachers, extremely stern and my mother always went to them to solve their problems (for example their children ran away from home). It was always them (my cousins) who were better, harder working, created more in their lives (in fact – they are now miserable, they actually have nothing) I always had to be like them. I always hated them, even nowadays I do not have any contact with them. On the other side – my father had a brother with two children, nobles, good pupils, sportsmen . . . I had to be like them as well. I do not have a contact with them either. VOICE – noise: Gossiping, and then my mother and father would quarrel – from my father side very 'fine' and well educated, opposite from my mother side . . . always many voices, that were not ours. If it wasn't for my mother's huge bond with her sister . . . maybe my mother and father would stay longer together.

My mother and father never had a common bedroom. I was once making spots with a stick on a freshly painted wall, my mother bit me so badly. She has never apologised to me. And so many times she was not right.

Stimulus word: Sick

I thought of not telling you but I will tell you. I got diagnosed with the breast cancer. I was in Belgrade at that time. When I went to oncology institute I wanted to die when I saw the cancer patients there. For quite a long while I did not want to do anything regarding the illness, just to let it go in its own course. Then I decided to go to Sweden. I stayed at my friend and his wife after the surgery and was on chemo therapy. It was tough but I made it. I was alone and nobody except my two best friends knew. I did not mind dying, just the pain. I had to be brave.

Everything will pass . . . I have to go on. If I stop I will get ill. The only thing that matters is that nobody looks at me.

Stimulus word: Pray

To pray for what. For health. Every time I was supposed to pray and light the candles I did, but . . . I am the one who can decide whether I will be ok or not. I do not understand people who find a church when they are not well. If I do not have peace with myself no church will help me. I do believe (not in priests), I am not a non-believer. I do not brag that I am a believer it is disgusting to me – bljak (like sljap). I do not believe that any of them is a true believer, it is all – mimicry.

BRAVE? – Me

Stimulus word: Marry

Nothing comes, but absolutely nothing. Point blank. I do not have a person, nor situation related to this. I do have a problem, guaranteed. Why when you marry, why do people always have incredible urge that now something needs to change. We are married now, now something needs to change. I fall in love with somebody with all the faults . . .

I wanted to change, but not somebody else changing me. I did change by my own will for somebody before . . . what came to me then! I would consciously stop myself wanting to change somebody, to adjust. My friend has a habit to chew a tooth-pick. My female friend, his partner keeps telling him – take the tooth-pick out, stop eating that much . . ., grumping, grumping or being angry and silent . . . that is marriage. A cage – because of this grumping. Returning the images of my mother and father and also some of my relationships. Why do I care . . . why one has to get married in order to be socially successful?! Are you married? – they ask me, and if I am not, it must be something wrong with me . . .

Stimulus word: Party

I simply cannot recall a party or wedding that I had a good time. Weddings – kitsch parades. Parties – it comes down to talking to people I came with, drinking beer and smoking dope. And if among those 50 people there is somebody 'smart' and starts talking . . ., I immediately get quiet. I like to go out, I like to get together over dinner and talk with my friends, but not with 50 people . . . I do love my birthday, I make it the way I like, gather people I like . . . At the parties everybody speaks at the same time, I can't properly hear anybody . . . I did not like the disco clubs either. Smaller circle of friends I like, I feel safe, people who will not mind if I spill something on me, drink a bit more . . . I love demonstrations. Anarchy. I love concerts. I would marry The Englishman tomorrow, because he was genuine. With him I have never felt him wanting to change me, or laugh at me if I say something silly. We could speak about everything. We laughed a lot, I always loved to go out with him. He did not like 50 people parties either. I did not have to make myself beautiful in order for him to like me. Happiness. Then I would define marriage as freedom and big space. If only I could have that feeling again – to be able to be quiet in peace, to be myself . . .

Stimulus word: Hurt

That somebody who is going to hurt you must be stupid. I do not understand how they have time to do these things – to hurt somebody. My father and my mother . . . such insults and bad words . . . What do I gain if I tell you, you are so ugly . . . And then they would put me in the middle and ask me who was right. I will tell you directly what I think or I will keep quiet. I think it is a total stupidity either if I allow somebody to hurt me – somebody who will say to me something like how could you allow yourself to be so fat . . . My father used to tell me all the time how stupid I was. My partner used to tell me that I was stupid and brought me to the point when I actually thought either that I was ignorant or really stupid. It was only when I met The Englishman . . . My partner apologised later, I understood that he was not feeling ok in general that it was not me. It is selfish that I feel better if I hurt you. It is not clear to me and I do not want it to be clear to me. And who am I to judge . . . I do not like when people insult somebody. I feel sadness and if it is really a bad insult I get angry and then I want justice to be done.

Stimulus word: Flower

Oh yes! Flowers associated me with the smile and then to the hippy sign. Everything related to flowers calms me down, I love to work with flowers. I love to have flowers, it is beautiful and gentle. Poppy seed flower, ever so gentle creature, the petals, you need to take care of them and then it rewards you with something so beautiful. I could not pick a poppy-seed flower, ever. There is a fairy tale related with a poppy seed flower . . . There is a fairytale . . . It closes in the morning and opens in the evening, there are 3 petals, does not last long, a few days, flower of May, sometimes September . . . Maiden's veil. Don't laugh, lasts long, burnt by the sun, I took it

138   *Appendix 1*

back in to the shade. I grow flowers, "prkos" (contempt) is my favorite plant. I never know what kind of flower will come up, plus you don't need to water it. It is so tender, you think it will die, but it is actually so endurable . . . flowers from lilac to white, entire spectrum.

The context interview is an opportunity for the client to elaborate, explore and explain the responses made to the stimulus words which have attracted significant numbers of complex indicators.

During this process, the client typically produces further layers of associations, albeit given mainly in sentences and ad hoc phrases. These are naturally and inevitably accompanied with a second layer of complex indicators. Some of these will be the same as or similar to the reactions to stimulus words during the first meeting. Rarely, others will be completely new, as the client might have forgotten their earlier responses. (While for the purposes of training and examination it is not strictly necessary to make a note of these, it can be of interest to explore this deeper layer further, and a method designed by the authors for doing this is explained).

In this version of the interpretation hypothesis the experimenter took an extra step. She looked briefly at the next layer of associations and selected those nouns or verbs or predicates which have occurred most frequently and which also carried the most libidinal charge as measured by the usual range of observable complex indicators. The latter observations were not taken formally, so as to give the experimenter a 'feel' of working analytically in an unmeasured session, but were retrospectively checked against the transcript. The accuracy of the word selection evidenced a degree of internalisation of the skill of observation and inference (identifying complexes) as a result of this second cycle of learning. In effect, the word association method has been used recursively to illuminate potential complexes in deeper layers of cognitive memory and (RIG) networks and to give weaker or stronger evidence of those already identified.

Flower 16
People 14
Mother 14
Father 11
Love 10
Free 8
Rules 5
Peace 6
Kiss 5

This not only provided the experimenter with a further data field upon which to build the hypothesis but also alerted her to the recursive multi-linear aspects of interpretation. Practically, it opened the gate to a simple method building the draft complex map, linking vertical and horizontal associations, as follows:

		Words presented at context interview by experimenter									
		Free	Kiss	Naked	Boss	Family	Sick	Pray	Marry	Party	Hurt	Flower
MMost-used CI words in context interview	Flower											16
	People		1	3		1		1	1	6	1	
	Mother			4		8			1		1	
	Father		2	2		5					2	
	Love	1				1			1	4		3
	Free	5		2						1		
	Rules	1			4							
	Peace	4						1		1		
	Kiss		5									

From this table it can be seen that the vertical columns Boss, Pray and Flower are not strongly cross-referenced in many of the other columns. Flower seems to represent a fairly isolated 'positive' complex. The vertical chains of association can be seen, as can the horizontal chains which show indirect linkages between the vertical chains.

For example, the word 'free' occurs five times in both vertical and horizontal columns. That is partly to be expected. It is analogous to the repetition of the stimulus word, and as we already know that free was identified as complex indicator, perhaps not much new information is presented. However, free also occurs in the 'naked' column and in the 'party' column, and so it suggests a thematic connection between 'free', 'naked' and 'party'. This becomes clearer when the syntax is examined.

Naked

No constraints, it associates me of that **free**dom, nothing is constraining me.
   I was frustrated I couldn't be me. My only **free**dom was when I was with an animal and did whatever I wanted with it.

Party

He did not like 50 people parties either. I did not have to make myself beautiful in order for him to like me. Happiness. Then I would define marriage as **free**dom and big space. If only I could have that feeling again – to be able to be quiet in peace, to be myself . . .

When one refers to first association to the word free, there are very striking similarities between these associations and the elaborations discovered in the cross-referencing, which clarifies meaning.

Furthermore, the indirect chains of association reveal quite some meaning when the final sentence of the associations to 'naked' are considered in yet another layer of context-providing associations.

   I had problems defecating (3–4 years of age). They made me sit on the potty for hours.
   Till 3 years ago, I was not able to empty my bowels regularly.

It is perhaps not difficult then to imagine how interpretation hypotheses can usefully be drawn from this process. The picture can be further clarified by repeating the procedure for all the words in the horizontal column.

The research method is recursive, reflexive and inductive, the object of which is to allow complexes to emerge from the material and to be expressed in the language of the client or patient.

The analysis begins to identify the network (as well as the chains) of associations, a concept which resonates strongly with Jung's theory of individuation, progression towards wholeness. Both in theory and practice, awareness of the deeper layers of association appear to have therapeutic benefit and diagnostic value.

Appendix 2
100-word list

Word Number	Stimulus Word	Reaction Time 5ths	Reaction Time Sec.	Reaction	Reproduction	Reaction Notes	Complex Indicator Types				CIs	Response Type	
							Over PM	Re	sounds	other		Factual	Egocentric
1	head												
2	green												
3	water												
4	sing												
5	dead												
6	long												
7	ship												
8	make												
9	woman												
10	friendly												
11	bake												
12	ask												
13	cold												
14	stalk												
15	dance												
16	village												
17	pond												
18	sick												
19	pride												
20	bring												
21	ink												
22	angry												
23	needle												
24	swim												
25	go												
26	blue												
27	lamp												
28	carry												
29	bread												
30	rich												
31	tree												
32	jump												
33	pity												
34	yellow												
35	street												
36	bury												
37	salt												
38	new												
39	habit												
40	pray												
41	money												
42	silly												
43	book												

(*Continued*)

Appendix 2 141

(Continued)

Word Number	Stimulus Word	Reaction Time 5ths	Reaction Time Sec.	Reaction	Reproduction	Reaction Notes	Complex Indicator Types				CIs	Response Type	
							Over PM	Re	sounds	other		Factual	Egocentric
44	despise												
45	finger												
46	jolly												
47	bird												
48	walk												
49	paper												
50	wicked												
51	frog												
52	try												
53	hunger												
54	white												
55	child												
56	speak												
57	pencil												
58	sad												
59	plum												
60	marry												
61	home												
62	nasty												
63	glass												
64	fight												
65	wool												
66	big												
67	carrot												
68	give												
69	doctor												
70	frosty												
71	flower												
72	beat												
73	box												
74	old												
75	family												
76	wait												
77	cow												
78	name												
79	luck												
80	say												
81	table												
82	naughty												
83	brother												
84	afraid												
85	love												
86	chair												
87	worry												
88	kiss												
89	bride												
90	clean												
91	bag												
92	choice												
93	bed												
94	pleased												
95	happy												
96	shut												
97	wound												
98	evil												
99	door												
100	insult												

Appendix 3
Global Assessment of Functioning (GAF) scale

(From DSM-IV-TR, p. 34.)

Consider psychological, social, and occupational functioning on a hypothetical continuum of mental health-illness. Do not include impairment in functioning due to physical (or environmental) limitations.

Code	(Note: Use intermediate codes when appropriate, e.g. 45, 68, 72.)
100 | 91	**Superior functioning in a wide range of activities, life's problems never seem to get out of hand, is sought out by others because of his or her many positive qualities. No symptoms.**
90 | 81	**Absent or minimal symptoms** (e.g. mild anxiety before an exam)**, good functioning in all areas, interested and involved in a wide range of activities. socially effective, generally satisfied with life, no more than everyday problems or concerns** (e.g. an occasional argument with family members).
80 | 71	**If symptoms are present, they are transient and expectable reactions to psychosocial stressors** (e.g. difficulty concentrating after family argument); **no more than slight impairment in social, occupational or school functioning** (e.g. temporarily failing behind in schoolwork).
70 | 61	**Some mild symptoms** (e.g. depressed mood and mild insomnia) **OR some difficulty in social, occupational, or school functioning** (e.g. occasional truancy, or theft within the household), **but generally functioning pretty well, has some meaningful interpersonal relationships**.
60 | 51	**Moderate symptoms** (e.g. flat affect and circumstantial speech, occasional panic attacks) **OR moderate difficulty in social, occupational, or school functioning** (e.g. few friends, conflicts with peers or co-workers).
50 | 41	**Serious symptoms** (e.g. suicidal ideation, severe obsessional rituals, frequent shoplifting) **OR any serious impairment in social, occupational, or school functioning** (e.g. no friends, unable to keep a job).
40 | 31	**Some impairment in reality testing or communication** (e.g. speech is at times illogical, obscure or irrelevant) **OR major impairment in several areas, such as work or school, family relations, judgement, thinking or mood** (e.g. depressed man avoids friends, neglects family and is unable to work; child frequently beats up younger children, is defiant at home and is failing at school).
30 | 21	**Behavior is considerably influenced by delusions or hallucinations OR serious impairment in communication or judgement** (e.g. sometimes incoherent, acts grossly inappropriately, suicidal preoccupation) **OR inability to function in almost all areas** (e.g. stays in bed all day; no job, home or friends).

20	**Some danger of hurting self or others** (e.g. suicide attempts without clear expectation of death; frequently violent; manic excitement)
|	**OR occasionally fails to maintain minimal personal hygiene** (e.g. smears feces)
11	**OR gross impairment in communication** (e.g. largely incoherent or mute).
10	**Persistent danger of severely hurting self or others** (e.g. recurrent violence)
|	**OR persistent inability to maintain minimal personal hygiene**
1	**OR serious suicidal act with clear expectation of death**.
0	Inadequate information.

Index

abandonment 90, 111, 112, 116
aetiology 112
affect 112
analysis: by complex indicator 13, 66; of feedback 62; Jungian 113; qualitative 69
analyst: 7; attitude 19; character of 7; client relationship 10; insights 52; interpretation 19; own projections and limitations 5; personal development 101; personal qualities 14; as sounding board 52; terms 103
anamnesis 14–20; aims 15; ancestors 16; birth order 15; childhood and youth 17; economic circumstances 17; education 17; example introduction 15–16; expectations 19; family and circumstances 18; guidance 14; occupations and interests 18; parents and carers 16; pervasive themes 18; significant events 18; significant problems 18; social context and climate 17; special characteristics of the Jungian anamnesis 19; stories, birth and early childhood 17
APA Committee on Nomenclature and Statistics 87
ARAS 3, 4
Aronson, J. 19
artificial intelligence 99, 106
borderline personality disorder 84

Bach, B. 87
Bertillon, J. 85
Beyer, C. 120
Bradley, M. 34

Cade, M. 95
Caire, M. 106
Casement, P. 97
chart: of complex indicators 65; function in Word 26; reaction times, make 26
common factor models: 98
complex indicator: analysis by 66; *codes and definitions* (*see* protocol); for complex map 43; developmental dynamics 56; libidinal charge 44; mistakes as 2; sensitization to 4; recording 10; soul 43; vital charge of images 43; sum of 22; video recording note 34; *see also* chart

complex: APA definition 12; aetiology and 89; applications in training 3–4; and DSM/ICD 49; ego complex differentiation 11; discovery of 2–3; emotional centres of 45; long standing 12; map (*see* map of complexes); loss of good authority 90; parental 11, 50, 92; post ego-formation 42; pre ego-formation 42; recording 34; RIGs and 63; selecting 33; snapshot of 12; structure of 44; theory 12; types of 45–46
context interview 33; example introduction 33; example of 35; guidance notes 33; interviewing method 34; research 41; video/audio recordings 34
counter-transference 23, 33, 49, 51, 57, 60, 61, 62, 69, 90, 91, 95, 98

Dalgleish, T. 91, 92, 94
Damasio, A. 96
diagnosis 117
differentiation 50, 118
DSM: assessment 89; example 89; hypothesis 49; key features 88; background of ICD 85–86, DSM 85, 87; overview 85; WAE and links to categories 88, 91; Word Association Experiment and DSM/ICD categories 85–91; *see also* ICD; transdiagnostic

Edinger, E. 66
Elkins, D. 97
emotion 46, 67, 71; as alchemical fire 119; feeling and 121; indicators of 34; measurement of 94, 95, 96
regulation of 107, 108; and thinking 106
empathy 21; fundamental connection 109; Husserl and 119; insula 107; intersubjectivity and 120; Stein on 96; in transference 129; *see also* Rogers
Escamilla, M. 54, 95, 130
examination: document 57–84; example document structure 12

Fierro, C. 96, 97
Folz, J. 34
Fractal 104–109, 120
Freese, H. 97

Index

GAF 143

Husserl, E. 119

individuation 7, 11, 13, 43, 57, 68, 72, 83, 98, 99, 101, 104, 105, 122, 123, 130, 139
interpretation 109
interpretation hypothesis 49–52

Jacoby, M. 53
Jaffe, A. 124
Jiang, Y. 108
Johnson, E. 42
Jung, C.G. early experimental research methods 1–2

Karsten, W. 42
Kast, V. 4, 23–25, 65, 69, 98, 99
Kawa, S. 87
Keiser, R.E. 26
Kent, H. 94

Langs, R. 97
learning guide, step-by-step 9
Lee, J. 4
Leichsenring, F. 88
Lepori, D. 42, 45, 50, 55, 71
letter of introduction 11
Lichtenberg, J. 53
limbic system 107, 108, 123

map of complexes 43–48; facts 43; internal relation of words, value and logic 44; landscapes 45; meaning 44; process 44; themes 44
Marks-Tarlow, T. 106
Marullo, C. 101
McGuire, W. 2
McLean hospital 91
meaning 3, 10, 114, 124, 139; alchemical term for 47; archetype of 54; collective and individual 74; false 56; Parsifal 48; recursive analysis and 134; in schizophrenia 42; symbolic 14
Meier, A. 32
Meier, C. A. 4
misuses 10

neurotransmitters 125
Nickerson, C. 95, 96

Oludare, A. 100

Papez, J.W 107
perseveration: in context interview 33; as *echo of emotion* 71; and recovery time 71; response reactions 70; trigger 73
Petchkovsky, L. 95
projection 127; analyst's own 50, 83; child 55; integration of 128; transference and 127–129

protocol 21; administer the AE using the template 23; AE template completed example 21; association types 30; calculations 25; chart, how to make 26; column headings and definitions 22; complex indicator codes and definitions 22; first 'administration' meeting 23; organise the data for analysis 25; perseverations 31; stereotypes 27
PTSD 17, 58, 108; assessment of 89–92; child maltreatment 93; undiagnosed 17

Queensland Brain Institute 125

Raminani, S. 85
recursive analysis 134
research 1–3, 8, 94–102; analytical psychology and psychiatry 109; archetypal 3; association 7; clinical 91; early experimental 1; emotions 93; ethics 11; in recursive analysis 134, 138–139; infant 9, 52; limits 91; meaninglessness 4; psychogenesis 6; software 134; transdiagnostic 91; validity 131; war 109
Roesler, C. 4, 89, 99
Rogers, C. 96, 97

Sadock, B. J. 107, 111, 126
schizophrenia 1–3, 8; association 109; diagnosis 109; meaninglessness 4; negative 10; positive and negative 42; psychogenesis 124; war 109
Schlegel, M. 5, 42
Schmidt, W. 19
self 53; core 54; emergent 53; remembering 56; senses of 53; subjective 54; verbal 55
Sharp, D. 113, 114, 116, 117, 121, 126, 127
Shono, Y. 99
Slade, T. 92
Smith, M. 132
Smith, W. 94, 121
Smolarski, D. 20
Stein, E. 96, 119
Stern,D. 37, 46, 52–54, 76, 96, 88
Szanto, T. 120

training: learning outcomes in 7–8; rationale and overview 6; 'rite of passage' in 7; scientific framework 6
transference 8, 50, 57, 60, 90, 117, 127–129; *see also* counter-transference
Tschuschke, V. 5, 42
Tuckman, B. 77
typology 129–130
Tyrer, P. 88

union of opposites: symbolic value as 7
uses 10; *see also* misuses

Vanden Bos, G. 111
Vieira, T. 120

WAE: therapeutic use of 50, 51
Wampold, B. 89, 97
Wang, F. 108
Ward, T. 99
Whitaker, B. 115
White, P. 114

WHO 85, 86
Winnicott, D. 55, 95
Witkowski, J. 99
Wundt, W. 112

Yakeley, J. 98